WHERE HAS
INTEGRITY
GONE?

REVISED EDITION

With Study Questions

Simon Schrock

Vision Publishers
Harrisonburg, VA

ISBN: 1-932676-08-2

Unless otherwise noted, all Scripture references are
from the **King James Version** of the Holy Bible.

Published by Vision Publishers
Harrisonburg, Virginia

Cover and Text Design: Lonnie D. Yoder
Editors: Timothy Kennedy, John D. Martin, John D. Risser
Digital Text Entry: Elizabeth B. Burkholder

For additional copies or comments write to:
Vision Publishers
P.O. Box 190
Harrisonburg, VA 22803
Phone: 877-488-0901
Fax: 540-437-1969
E-mail: orders@vision-publishers.com
www.vision-publishers.com
(see order forms in back)

Table of Contents

Contributors to Questions

Todd E. Neuschwander
Goshen, Indiana

Earl R. Delp
Harrisonburg, Virginia

Terrill Yoder
New Paris, Indiana

Lonnie Beachy
Plain City, Ohio

David E. Showalter
Irwin, Ohio

Ernest Hochstetler
Abbeville, South Carolina

Walter Beachy
Plain City, Ohio

Timothy Kennedy
Newville, Pennsylvania

Foreword

A SMALL CABINET HUNG ON THE WALL ABOVE THE WATER-ing trough for the farm animals. Bottles of various tonics and preparations for animals were kept in the cabinet. One day a boy, old enough to know better, poured some contents of one bottle into the water in the trough. When the boy's father discovered it, he asked his son if he had done it. The son lied, saying he had not poured the poison into the water. But the father discovered his son had lied, and he gave the boy appropriate discipline.

I was that boy. That experience taught me the terrible-ness of lying and that lying is not a laughing matter. In fact, it was a hurting matter. Many times since, I have been thankful for my father's discipline.

If you are serious about living a life of integrity, the message of this book will encourage you and strengthen your conviction to continue to "denounce the hidden things of dishonesty."

If you are caught in a habit of dishonesty, read on. This book will help you repent of your sin and live a life of integrity.

Perchance, dear reader, you have not been taught to live with integrity or to acknowledge the sinfulness of dishonesty. Open your mind and heart to the message of this book—a message based on the teachings of the One who will some day be our judge. Because He, the Lord Jesus, will judge us by His Word, it is our great privilege to know His teachings and live by them, so that we can enter into His glorious presence.

Preface

HAVE YOU EVER HEARD PEOPLE BRAG ABOUT HOW THEY "fibbed" a little and got the best end of a deal? The storyteller makes himself look like the smart guy and the victim the dummy. This kind of story you might hear at the local "coffee hole," where people gather to sip coffee and exchange gossip laced with tales that bring eruptions of laughter around the table. One man tells of fibbing to the police officer and getting out of a ticket. Another boasts of collecting a little extra insurance by pointing to prior damage on a vehicle—damage that was not part of the accident being investigated. Someone relates that he bought a gift for his girlfriend and claimed it as a business expense.

In an interview on Fox News, a well-known, influential newscaster told the nation, "You can be an honest person and lie about any number of things."[1] Lying and cheating have become common practice for many people. Is this a laughing matter, or does it represent a serious decline in moral standards? Is dishonesty just a clever way to get ahead, or will it lead to a bitter harvest for our society?

In the first several pages of the Bible we read the account of Satan deceiving the first couple. From that point on, lying has been present with the human race. The last pages of the Bible tell us where unrepentant liars will spend eternity. Between these opening and closing pages of the Bible are numerous accounts of people lying and some of the consequences. There are a few accounts of dishonesty in which God caused lying to work in His favor.[2] He can make evil ultimately defeat itself and work for good. I do not profess to know all the reasons that God works as He does, but the Bible tells us that "the times of this ignorance God winked at; but now commandeth all men everywhere to repent."[3]

Willful, deliberate lying is serious in the eyes of God. God sent His Son to be our Savior, to forgive us all our sins, and to empower us to live holy lives of honesty and integrity.

Once, I ordered and paid for a fish sandwich and a drink at Burger King*. When I opened the bag, I found an order of fries, too. I looked at my receipt to confirm that I had not paid for fries. I went back to the man who took the order and explained that I had fries I had not paid for. When it finally registered with him, he said the fries were on him. Another customer who had heard the exchange came to me and said, "It's refreshing to see honesty."

Through God's power, it is possible to live a life of honesty and integrity. Such a life is refreshing to God and the people around us.

Simon Schrock

---

1. *Washington Times,* "Dan on Bill," May 17, 2001.
2. Rahab in Joshua 2.
3. Acts 17:30.

CHAPTER ONE

We Live in a Dishonest World

AN EPIDEMIC OF LYING HAS SWEPT OVER OUR LAND. Our culture is shaped around the assumption that Americans are a dishonest and lying people. People must always be cautious to avoid being cheated. Businesses make huge efforts to screen out the liars and cheaters. Older people frequently talk of those "good old" days when a person's "yes" meant "yes" and "no" meant "no." A neighbor's word and handshake could be trusted. The customer could ask the merchant to charge it "till the end of the month." The businessman could "write it up" on an invoice and did not need to worry whether he would be paid. The farmer could hurry to the hardware store for a bolt, put it on his account, and get back to plowing. At one time, honesty and trust prevailed in our culture.

However, that has changed. Ours has become a culture of liars.

Lying has become a serious problem, aggravated by the prevailing attitude that everybody does it; therefore, it is not so bad. Some even claim one must lie these days to make it. Some business people say they must lie to stay in business. Public officials argue that those in government have a right to lie.

People have largely lost their awareness of the sinfulness of lying. We have lost sight of its consequences and the harvest that comes with it. For some, lying has become almost as natural as walking. The shame of being a liar has evaporated. As William Bennett once said, "Shame is synonymous with conscience. If you have no sense of shame, it means you have no sense of wrongdoing."[1]

Lying and dishonesty have become a way of life. The businessman lies to make an extra dollar. The employee lies on his time card. The manager lies to her employees. The husband lies to his wife about his unfaithfulness, and the wife lies to her husband. Parents lie to children, children to parents and others in leadership and authority.

People pose as salesmen offering a bargain, but underneath lies a carefully planned rip-off. The flyer in the mail poses as an advertisement of a legitimate company with a fantastic product; but it only represents a mailing address to receive your money. The salesperson is a fake planning a robbery. The list could go on and on.

People around the globe remember the image of an American President facing his country, angrily wagging his finger, and saying, "I did not." The truth is he did. In 1998, the chief law enforcement officer of the United States looked the people in the eye and lied. Instead of an "honest Abe" for President, Americans had a "lying Bill."

For many people, lying is simply a way of life. The only

bad part of it is getting caught. We have become a society of liars and a culture of dishonesty.

Years ago, my uncle from North Carolina came to Northern Virginia with the mission of seeing his congressman. Because he was older than 80 years, I thought I should go with him to Capitol Hill. He believed airplane jet streams were evidence that someone was seeding the clouds to make it rain. He wanted to ask his congressman to check into the matter and put a stop to it. We arrived at the congressman's office, and Uncle inquired about seeing his representative. The secretary gave her "I'm sorry, he is not here right now" speech. Uncle did not accept that very gracefully. He let her know he had come all the way from North Carolina and wanted to see the man. Within minutes we were ushered to his office, into the presence of the congressman who was there after all. "He is not here right now" is a common lie used nonchalantly.

I remember a conversation from my days of working at a hospital in Washington, D.C. We had to spend a lot of time cleaning and sharpening needles. This allowed for conversation. One of the discussions was about being in a street car accident. Someone said that if you are involved in an accident, you should claim a back injury. Even if you do not have an injury, no one can prove your back does not hurt and you can collect insurance money.

Our company, Choice Books, uses vans to deliver our books to retail stores. When we replace an old van, we often put it in our parking lot with a "for sale" sign on it.

Once, a brown van was on our lot to sell, and a potential buyer stopped to see it, inquiring about the price. There were several people in the interested party. They claimed that they needed the van to transport handicapped children. Their appeal to us was that they would use it to help others, so God would bless us if we sold it to them at their price. Eventually, we decided to let them have the van at the reduced price they offered.

Several days later, one of our associates drove past a shopping center and noticed this van in the parking lot for sale. He wrote down the phone number that was posted on the van and called for information. The person who answered the call claimed to have owned the van for years, declaring it to be in better condition than it really was, and said it had a rebuilt engine. When my associate identified himself, the buyer claimed we had sold them a bad van. This man freely lied to buy the van and lied just as easily to try and sell it.

For many, lying has become a way of life. A Washington merchant hung this sign in his shop window: "You can fool some people some of the time, and generally speaking, that's enough to allow for profit."[2]

Words from the Bible describe our lying condition.

> Now the Spirit speaketh expressly, that in the latter times some shall depart from the faith, giving heed to seducing spirits, and doctrines of devils; Speaking lies in hypocrisy; having their conscience seared with a hot iron (1 Timothy 4:1, 2).

This Scripture warns that people will fall away from the faith and pay attention to deceiving spirits and doctrines taught by demons. These deceivers teach false doctrine through their hypocritical lying. They can do this because their conscience is seared, and they can no longer distinguish right from wrong. Their conscience is silent about lying.

Look around you! We live in a lying world. Dishonesty has become so pervasive that even people in the church lie. People who claim to be God's children and sing hymns on Sunday morning also are caught in the lying web.

I recall watching a minister's wife arrange a dozen eggs in order to slip in some smaller ones and make it still look like a dozen large eggs. She arranged a lie.

I read once of a preacher who took a $450 deduction on his tax return for a "clerical collar." Despite the increase in the cost of living, this seemed a little out of line to IRS officials. The minister was called to give an account. He claimed an honest mistake. The $450 should have been $4.50. The understanding IRS men let the preacher pay the extra tax plus 5% interest. "But one shrewd auditor had a second guess. Sure enough, a scrutiny of past income tax returns showed that the minister consistently had trouble with decimals. For three years in a row, things such as $4.50 came out $450 in the deductions column. For this, the red-faced cleric paid added taxes, 6% interest, and a 50% penalty for fraud."[3] I cannot imagine that the IRS agents would have picked this preacher to instruct them in the ways of godliness.

Once, a letter addressed to Resident came in the mail. "TO A FRIEND" was written in the mailing address.

Above the address it read, "PRIVATE & CONFIDEN-TIAL." Big letters across the envelope claimed, "God's Holy Spirit said, 'Someone connected with this address needs help.' " Inside it declared, "GOD'S HOLY SPIRIT IS IN AND ON THIS HOLY LETTER." The letter, with yellow highlights, continued: "Please read this urgent word in the spirit that came to us concerning you or someone connected with this address. . . . We see something leaving heaven, heading towards you. . . . God said, 'Tell someone at this address that I am ready to break the financial curse that has had a hold on matters so pressing.' "

The letter went on to say that the sender had enclosed a "biblical contact." It was a piece of fabric, red on one side and gold on the other. The red was in honor of the blood of Jesus, and the gold was to represent one's finances.

According to the instructions, the red and gold biblical contact was to be placed under the receiver's pillow at night. Then, the red and gold biblical contact was to be returned to the sender to be kept as a personal contact for the receiver, when the sender prayed. Further instructions said that it should be placed under the pillow inside the receiver's wallet. "That is your point of Bible faith contact to break the financial curse that troubles your money matters," the sender wrote. The letter also promised a "new beginning in the realm of the spirit, for it will be a new birth."

Then the letter got to the point. "As soon as possible, go and place this red and gold biblical contact under your pillow (inside your wallet) as you sleep tonight. In the morning, place it on top of your prove-God sacrificial seeding offering of $5, $10, $20 or another amount that God leads you to."

There was a blank to check which said, "Yes, I am sowing a prove-God, Malachi 3:10 seed offering of (____) to break any curses, especially any financial curses, that hinder me." The letter was signed, "St. Matthew 18:19."

I can imagine poor widows giving of their meager incomes, expecting a rich return from God. Swindlers pose as ministers of the gospel, but they are only padding their pockets. Preachers parade on stages "preaching the gospel," but lie to those around them about their whereabouts as they carry on adulterous relationships. Others fabricate drives to help the poor, so that they can increase their own wealth. Singers pose as representatives of the Lord, when inside they really aim to become stars.

Jesus warned of religious deception and lying:

Beware of false prophets, which come to you in sheep's clothing, but inwardly they are ravening wolves (Matthew 7:15).

Beware of preachers or organizations that are not open about who they are. Beware of mailings that sound Christian but provide no number to call and furnish no evidence of financial accountability. We are surrounded by religious fakes flowing with the lying stream like dead fish in a river.

This calls for a serious look into the source of truth— God's Word. Lying is a gross violation of God's teaching. When you lie, you sin against God. Very early in the history of God's people, He forbade lying. In the Old Testament, lying was strictly forbidden.

> Ye shall not steal, neither deal falsely, neither lie one to another (Leviticus 19:11).

The New Testament commandment is just as strong.

> But now ye also put off all these; anger, wrath, malice, blasphemy, filthy communication out of your mouth. Lie not one to another, seeing that ye have put off the old man with his deeds (Colossians 3:8, 9).

To build a conviction against lying and to keep our consciences sharp, we need to be reminded again and again of what God's Word teaches. Here are a few reminders from the Bible:

- Be fair when you judge people. And be fair when you measure and weigh things. Your weighing baskets should be the right size. And your jars should hold the right amount of liquid. Your weights and balances should weigh correctly. I am the Lord your God. I brought you out of the land of Egypt (Leviticus 19:35-36, NCV).[4]

David made a commitment of integrity in his psalms.

- Mine eyes shall be upon the faithful of the

land, that they may dwell with me: he that walketh in a perfect way, he shall serve me. He that worketh deceit shall not dwell within my house: he that telleth lies shall not tarry in my sight. I will early destroy all the wicked of the land; that I may cut off all wicked doers from the city of the Lord (Psalm 101:6–8).

Solomon wrote numerous proverbs calling attention to integrity and honesty.

- These six things doth the Lord hate: yea, seven are an abomination unto him: a proud look, a lying tongue, and hands that shed innocent blood, an heart that deviseth wicked imaginations, feet that be swift in running to mischief, a false witness that speaketh lies, and he that soweth discord among brethren (Proverbs 6:16–19).

- A false balance is abomination to the Lord: but a just weight is his delight (Proverbs 11:1).

- Lying lips are abomination to the Lord: but they that deal truly are his delight (Proverbs 12:22).

- A righteous man hateth lying: but a wicked man is loathsome, and cometh to shame (Proverbs 13:5).

- A just weight and balance are the Lord's: all

the weights of the bag are his work (Proverbs 16:11).

- A false witness shall not be unpunished, and he that speaketh lies shall not escape (Proverbs 19:5).

- The desire of a man is his kindness: and a poor man is better than a liar (Proverbs 19:22).

- The getting of treasures by a lying tongue is a vanity tossed to and fro of them that seek death (Proverbs 21:6).

A prophet of God declared the Lord's hatred for false oaths.

- These are the things that ye shall do; speak ye every man the truth to his neighbour; execute the judgment of truth and peace in your gates: And let none of you imagine evil in your hearts against his neighbour; and love no false oath: for all these are things that I hate, saith the LORD (Zechariah 8:16,17).

Paul reminds the church to put away lying and speak the truth.

- But speaking the truth in love, may [we] grow up into him in all things, which is the head, even Christ (Ephesians 4:15).

- Wherefore putting away lying, speak every man truth with his neighbour: for we are members one of another (Ephesians 4:25).

The clear message from God is that we must speak the truth and that God hates the sin of lying. God's Word teaches us not to lie one to another.

Let the truth of God's Word strengthen your conscience that lying is wrong and that His children should speak the truth.

This word is from the book of Hebrews:

Pray for us: for we trust we have a good conscience, in all things willing to live honestly (Hebrews 13:18).

---

1. *The Washington Times,* March 16, 1995.
2. *Encyclopedia of 7700 Illustrations,* Assurance Press.
3. *Encyclopedia of 7700 Illustrations,* Assurance Press.
4. New Century Version.

Questions for Discussion

1. Much of the dishonesty that we see today is a symptom of a deeper problem. What are root causes of current dishonesty?

2. Think of a time when you were misled. What did it do to you? How did it make you feel? Compare this to a time when you misled someone. What did this do to the person? What did it do to your relationship?

3. Is it ever wrong to misrepresent the truth so that a greater good may be accomplished? What are ways that we depersonalize the sin of lying?

4. What attitudes in contemporary culture aggravate the problem of dishonesty in our society?

5. List several ways you can strengthen your conscience against lying.

CHAPTER TWO

Lying—It's Not a Laughing Matter!

Have you ever heard someone boast of getting an advantage over another person by shading the truth and being "a little" dishonest? Have you ever listened to a clever story about using dishonesty to avoid consequences and heard a ripple of laughter spread through the group? One person shortchanges another, and the tale quickly becomes a favorite lunchroom joke!

Ah—some say, we do it all the time! Students use a little untruth to outwit a teacher. Motorists quickly make up false excuses for speeding. The church member scrambles to arrange words so that his statement may not be called "lies."

A Florida newspaper carried an article entitled "Fast-thinking Speeders Often Leave Truth and Reality in Dust."[1] The article contained excuses that drivers often give to the police. One speeder claimed he was being chased by deer and declared that he was trying to outrun them!

An old church bishop once told the story of a person who had a forbidden item in his possession. When the person was approached about the matter, he responded by saying he had "stuck it in the stove," implying that he had burned the item. However, the stove had no fire in it! The words were true; the intent of the heart was misleading.

Polls taken during President Clinton's impeachment trial in 1999 indicated that about 65% of Americans did not consider lying to be a very serious offense. They believed the President lied, but that it was not something to get upset about, nor a reason to remove him from office. After all, the economy was good—what did a little lying hurt?

In a news article titled "Bearing False Witness to Thy Pollster," the report says,

> Social scientists have suspected for years that people fib when pollsters ask them about their church-going habits. One big reason for this scholarly skepticism is that the proportion of Americans who say they go to church at least once a week has not changed in three decades: Year in and year out, four in 10 Americans say they went.
>
> Now, two researchers have tapped a novel source—thousands of times-use diaries completed in the mid-1960s, 1970s and 1990s—in an attempt to find out how often Americans really go to church.
>
> Their analysis reveals a discrepancy between the diaries and the polls, which suggests that

many Americans have been misreporting how they spend their Sunday mornings, inflating estimates of church attendance by perhaps as much as a third.

What's more, the number of Americans who apparently lie about their church-going habits is increasing, says sociologist Stanley Presser of the University of Maryland and his research partner, Linda Stinson of the U.S. Bureau of Labor Statistics.

Based on their analysis of the diaries, they determined that the percentage of Americans who attended church the previous week plummeted from 42 percent in 1965 to 26 percent in 1994. "That's a 16 percentage-point fall off, which is really very striking," Presser said.[2]

Both the Clinton polls and the diaries are revealing. They demonstrate that many people see lying as a laughing matter, not a serious concern.

Why bother to address the subject of lying? Doesn't almost everybody do it? Lying is a way of life, and the world still turns and the sun rises on schedule. What's the problem?

Lying Has Consequences

Imagine a little old grandma shaking her gnarled arthritic finger at her young grandson and saying, "Listen, son, lyin' don't pay!"

One memory of my early childhood is the leather strap that hung on a nail behind the heating stove. I have no memories of any abuse from that piece of leather, but I know that it represented consequences.

Many of us in the older generation can tell stories of the consequences of dishonesty. In my own early childhood, it was deeply impressed on my mind that lying was major disobedience. Lying was a serious sin. It was displeasing to God. Therefore, lying had consequences. For many, the consequence was a form of discipline that brought correction. Fortunate children learned that lying has stinging consequences. The short-lived pain of correction during childhood is indeed a blessing, compared to the bitter consequences that follow adult liars.

Lying still brings bitter consequences. When lying is carried into adulthood, the painful results are compounded. President Clinton's lying in the 1990s provides an example of the costly outgrowth of lying. It cost the American taxpayers 40 million dollars to investigate and uncover the President's lies, and it cost millions more to try to cover them up.

But money is not the most serious consequence of deception. By lying, the President added to the shameful Lewinsky affair. The conflicting images of the President walking out of church with a big Bible in his hand and then lying before a grand jury mocked true Christianity, which teaches that lying is sin.

People were hurt, relationships were shattered, derogatory names were hurled, and characters were attacked.

Blame was shifted to innocent people. Those who had lied blamed the prosecutors for the affair. The chief liar's chief attorney tried to put the blame on a decent, law-abiding, taxpaying, church-going prosecutor.

Decency, morality, righteousness, and respect for law took a beating because of this lying and deceit in high places of authority. These are just a few of the bitter consequences of lying.

The Bible declares well that:

Righteousness exalteth a nation: but sin is a reproach to any people (Proverbs 14:34).

The sin of lying has brought reproach and disgrace to our nation. The bitter consequences continue to play themselves out like seashells washing onto the beach. We will be reaping them for years to come. A simple telling of the truth would have avoided these consequences.

Lying Shapes a Culture

The bulletin of the Better Business Bureau explains why the bureau exists.

Monitoring advertising was one of the first marketplace issues that the Bureau system tackled when Bureaus first began to form in the early 1900s. In fact, the issue of 'truthfulness in advertising' served as the very spark which started the Better Business Bureau. Since then, standards of advertising in the U.S. have seen a huge swing toward what we now enjoy today, for the most part, as an environment geared toward accurate and reasonable advertising practices.[3]

Businesses are not always truthful in their advertising. Each weekday, the Bureau reviews the newspapers in the Washington area. They look for ads that do not meet the Bureau's standard for honest advertising. If they find something that may be misleading, they contact the advertiser.

We must all stay alert to the possibility of being cheated. I'm glad the Better Business Bureau works for truthfulness in advertising. Someone needs to uphold standards of truthfulness and honesty. But this is yet another cost of lying: we must pay people and organizations to keep watch, lest the people are deceived.

Lying, cheating, dishonesty—anything but just straight honesty—changes the lifestyle of a community and a nation. To survive we must make laws, provide enforcement officers, and "beef up" security.

A recent experience with a law enforcement officer at the Pentagon reminded me of this. Choice Books has serviced a bookrack at the Pentagon for more than thirty years. Getting in to service the rack was rather simple in the earlier years. Then came the concern about terrorism. Barricades went up, and busses and commercial vehicles could no longer pass under the building. Security has been "beefed up" many times since then.

One cool morning, with the sun shining brightly on an unexpected accumulation of snow, I was on my way to service the Pentagon rack. I exited the highway toward the south entrance and parking lot. I carefully stopped at the first stop sign and moved on toward the security checkpoint and the entrance to the loading dock. However, security checks were heightened. This meant that before approaching the security gate, I had to make a left turn and go several blocks to a station to have the vehicle checked. I saw where I needed to turn and proceeded to do so. As I was making the turn, I latently realized I had run a stop sign. About that time I heard a siren, which confirmed my error.

How embarrassing! This was not a big crime. It wouldn't take long. I pulled over and stopped. The officer stopped behind me. I got out my license and waited for the officer to come to my door. However, the officer did not get out of her car. She just sat there. So did I. After what seemed like a long wait, I got out of my van. Through a loud-speaker she ordered me to get back inside the van. So, I sat and waited some more.

After a few minutes, another officer drove up behind me. Then both officers got out of their vehicles, one on each side, and cautiously walked toward my van. I rolled down the windows of both doors to allow them full access to air their grievances. She reminded me of my offense, got my license and registration, and went back to her car. After what seemed like a long time, she served me with a $60.00 fine.

Part of me felt that I was being treated like a serious criminal. If she only knew! I was a law-abiding citizen who would do her no harm.

Imagine the scene! Here was a church bishop stopped on the south side of the Pentagon, two police cars with lights flashing, and two police officers cautiously approaching him from both sides of the vehicle.

Really, though, I do understand. We live in a lying, violent culture. How would the officer know that this van truly represented what the magnetic signs said? She did not know if this was a fake identity, hiding a different reality within the van. She did not know I was ready to cooperate fully.

After I received my ticket, I pulled away through the next intersection, stopping at all stop signs! I arrived at the place where the vehicle was to be checked. I was ordered to turn around and go back to the dock. One officer walked around with a mirror on a long handle, inspecting the vehicle underneath. Another officer opened the back door and asked questions. Still another officer checked his computer to see if my vehicle was registered in the system. After passing these checks, I was given a red card with the time printed on it. A clip was fastened to my mirror frame. I was told that I had only ten minutes to get back to the security gate at the Pentagon.

Finally, I arrived back at the gate. The gate lifted, and I drove through to the guard house. The officer saw the metal clip, registered the red card, and kept my driver's license while I was doing my business at the bookstore.

I am not complaining about the system. I share my experience to illustrate the extent to which officials must go to keep people posing as friends from carrying out acts of violence. While I was waiting to receive my red card and clip at the vehicle check station, I counted a dozen people around the dock and inside the building. Imagine the tax money it takes to filter out liars and crooks!

The consequences of a lying society can also be felt at the airport. An innocent-looking briefcase left in an airport restroom may be a bomb instead of a forgotten personal item.

An individual suffers the consequences of widespread deception when he gets his driver's license, goes to the bank, or makes a major purchase on credit.

Our ministry uses a number of vehicles to carry on the work. This means buying vehicles for our use and selling the ones we replace. The transaction of vehicles requires a mileage disclosure upon transfer of ownership. Both the seller and the buyer must sign the disclosure.

On the disclosure form, the opening statement reads:

Federal law (and State law, if applicable) requires that you state the mileage upon transfer of ownership. Failure to complete or providing a false statement may result in fines and/or imprisonment.

Why an extra form with signatures just to sell or buy a car? Because lying about mileage has become an all-too-common practice. Dishonesty requires enacting more laws, creating more forms and more work, for which *someone* has to pay.

The consequences of lying and dishonesty affect even the economy of a nation. If only liars could realize their actions are making life harder for themselves and for everyone else.

Lying doesn't pay—it costs tremendously. Proverbs 21:6 addresses the consequences of lying.

> The getting of treasures by a lying tongue is a fleeting vapor, the pursuit of death (Proverbs 21:6, NASB).

The little old grandmother is absolutely right when she sternly shakes her pointed finger at her little grandson and says, "Listen, son, lyin' don't pay." Lying doesn't pay. It has a price tag so big, humanity cannot even calculate the cost.

Lying Is a Big Deal to God

Lying is serious in the eyes of God. What man passes off with a shrug of the shoulders saying, "no big deal," God calls an abomination.

> Lying lips are abomination to the LORD: but they that deal truly are his delight (Proverbs 12:22).

> Lying lips are extremely disgusting and hateful to the LORD (Proverbs 12:22, *Amplified Bible*).

> A false balance and unrighteous dealings are extremely offensive and shamefully sinful to the LORD (Proverbs 11:1, *Amplified Bible*).

Proverbs 6:16-19 says there are six things God hates. One of them is "a false witness who breathes out lies [even under oath] . . ." (Proverbs 6:19, *Amplified Bible*).

A New Testament Scripture tells us how seriously God looks at lying. Take special note of this account in Acts 5:1–11.

> Now a man named Ananias, together with his wife Sapphira, also sold a piece of property. With his wife's full knowledge he kept back part of the money for himself, but brought the rest and put it at the apostles' feet.
>
> Then Peter said, "Ananias, how is it that Satan has so filled your heart that you have lied to the Holy Spirit and have kept for yourself some of the money you received for the land? Didn't it belong to you before it was sold? And after it was sold, wasn't the money at your disposal? What made you think of doing such a thing? You have not lied to men but to God."
>
> When Ananias heard this, he fell down and died. And great fear seized all who heard what had happened. Then the young men came forward, wrapped up his body, and carried him out and buried him.
>
> About three hours later his wife came in, not knowing what had happened. Peter asked her, "Tell me, is this the price you and Ananias got for the land?"
>
> "Yes," she said, "that is the price."
>
> Peter said to her, "How could you agree to test the Spirit of the Lord? Look! The feet of the men

who buried your husband are at the door, and they will carry you out also."

At that moment she fell down at his feet and died. Then the young men came in and, finding her dead, carried her out and buried her beside her husband. Great fear seized the whole church and all who heard about these events (Acts 5:1–11, NIV).

Lying is a serious matter with God. God does make a big deal over lying.

God does not knock everyone over these days for lying. If He did, there would be a lot of dead to bury. However, He gave us this example to tell us emphatically what He thinks of it. It should be a lesson for people of all ages. The record clearly communicates that God hates lying. Liars today do not receive instant judgment, as did Ananias and Sapphira. However, all liars who do not repent and receive God's forgiveness shall receive justice at the judgment. That is not a laughing matter.

Lying Destroys Discernment

What is so serious about lying? It has serious consequences for the liar. A person who practices lying can come to the point of believing his own lies.

The Bible teaches that lying is sinful and disgraceful. Churches have taught that lying is wrong. Parents teach their children that it is wrong. Schoolteachers reinforce the same message. As a result, many people have developed a conscience against lying. Thus, when lying seems to offer a temporal benefit, the conscience says "no!" The conscience brings a warning signal to not lie.

However, if a person ignores that signal and continues lying, the conscience will become dull. Every deliberate lie works at making the conscience ineffective.

Notice what the Bible says:

> Now the Spirit speaketh expressly, that in the latter times some shall depart from the faith, giving heed to seducing spirits, and doctrines of devils; Speaking lies in hypocrisy; having their conscience seared with a hot iron; Forbidding to marry, and commanding to abstain from meats which God hath created to be received with thanksgiving of them which believe and know the truth (1 Timothy 4:1-3).

Both listening to error and lying burn the sensitive receptors of the conscience, which then becomes hard and unfeeling, like scarred tissue. The conscience is seared, made of no effect; it no longer convicts. To lie until the conscience is seared and dull is a serious matter. It is so serious that God sends strong delusions, and liars believe lies.

First Timothy tells us that some shall "depart from the faith." They will stop believing God and His Word. Instead, they will turn to deceitful spirits and doctrines taught by demons. Instead of believing and following the Word of God, they will obey lying spirits.

Such teaching comes from hypocrites who cannot see right from wrong because their understanding has been destroyed with a hot iron. Their conscience is seared. They have rejected the truth and followed the lies of demons for so long that their own consciences no longer convict.

> And for this cause God shall send them strong delusion, that they should believe a lie: that they all might be damned who believed not the truth, but had pleasure in unrighteousness (2 Thessalonians 2:11, 12).

Here is the real tragedy: God will enable people who do not love and believe the truth to believe lies. It is therefore a momentous matter to tell lies, to act out lies, and to live a life of dishonesty.

Lying is a choice that people make. God recognizes that choice and allows a person to be a liar. When a person makes that choice, he then believes his own untruth and will be damned and perish in his own unrighteousness. They "will be judged guilty".[4] That is not a laughing matter.

---

1. "Fast-thinking Speeders Often Leave Truth, Reality in Dust," *Sarasota Herald Tribune,* January 12, 1998.
2. "Bearing False Witness to Thy Pollster," *The Washington Post,* May 17, 1998.
3. "Bureau Steps Up Ad Review Program," *The Bureau Bulletin,* January/February, 1999, Volume 2, Issue 4, page 2.
4. 2 Thessalonians 2:12, NCV.

Questions for Discussion

1. How should we react to someone telling a "humorous" story based on a lie?
2. What are some consequences of lying?
3. How does lying help to shape the culture in which we live?
4. What does God think about lying? Give some Scriptures to illustrate.
5. What are some ways that will help us see lying the way God sees it?
6. If a Christian does not see the seriousness of lying, or seems to find humor in stories revolving around lies, what does this say about the person's life? 1 Corinthians 2:14; 3:1-3; 14:20; Romans 8:6.
7. How does lying affect one's ability to recognize truth?

CHAPTER THREE

Lying Escalates Evil

L YING IS LIKE STEPPING ON THE DOWN SIDE OF AN esca-lator. It only goes in one direction. Lying creates an effect like the Vietnam War did for America. What started as a small involvement escalated into a long war of bombing and daily casualties. Eventually, Vietnam divided the nation and brought chaos on the home front. Lying works that way. It escalates evil.

Notice what Romans 1:18 says about the seriousness of repressing and hindering the truth.

> For God's (holy) wrath and indignation are revealed from heaven against all ungodliness and unrighteousness of men, who in their wickedness repress and hinder the truth and make it inoperative *(Amplified Bible)*.

Suppressing and hindering the truth is a serious matter. Step by step it increases evil. Romans 1:18-32 continues, listing dishonesty's downward steps.

- People suppress the truth by wickedness.

- They know the truth and therefore are without excuse.
- They do not glorify God or give thanks to Him.
- Instead, they become godless in their thinking.
- Then they exchange the glory of God for the worship of idols. They trade God's glory for things that look like animals, birds, and snakes.
- They desire more and more to do evil.
- Therefore God gives them over in the lusts of their hearts to impurity, that their bodies might be dishonored among them. For they exchanged the truth of God for a lie, and worshiped and served the creature rather than the Creator, who is blessed forever. Amen (Romans 1:24, 25, NASB).

They exchanged the truth of God for a lie. Because of this, God gave them over to shameful lusts.

They have become filled with every kind of wickedness (Romans 1:29, NIV).

This seems a fitting description of our culture! Rejecting and suppressing the truth, we are on a downward escalator, descending into "every kind of wickedness."

The downward spiral of lying is illustrated by Saul's life. God instructed Saul to destroy Amalek, to "utterly destroy all that they have, and spare them not." He was ordered specifically to destroy all of the Amalekites' cattle.

But Saul and his people spared King Agag, and the best of the Amalekites' sheep, oxen, fatlings, and lambs. All that was good, Saul did not destroy.

Saul failed to obey the commands of God, so God sent the prophet Samuel to confront Saul about his disobedience. Notice Saul's response:

> Blessed be thou of the Lord: I have performed the commandment of the Lord (1 Samuel 15:13).

King Saul lied! He had not fully obeyed the Lord. Consequently, Samuel asked the meaning of the animals he heard mooing and bleating.

Saul went on down the escalator to more evil. After being caught in his lie, he tried to blame someone else.

> And Saul said, They have brought them from the Amalekites: for the people spared the best of the sheep and of the oxen, to sacrifice unto the Lord thy God; and the rest we have utterly destroyed (1 Samuel 15:15).

Not only did he blame his people for doing it: he descended to suggesting his disobedience was meant to honor God with sacrifices. First it was a lie, then blame-shifting, then a false posturing of piety.

Saul then put on a phony repentance act. He explained that he did it because he feared the people. He did admit he had made a mistake, but then he suggested to Samuel that the prophet should make Saul look good before the people.

Saul answered, "I have sinned. But please honor me in front of my peoples' older leaders. Please honor me in front of the Israelites. Come back with me so that I may worship the Lord your God" (1 Samuel 15:30, NCV).

Saul did not truly repent before the Lord. He justified and covered up. The downward escalator kept going.

Later, Saul was overtaken with jealousy when David was honored for killing Goliath. He descended to anger, suspicion, fear, and an evil spirit. He concocted an evil plot to murder David. He spent much of his later life searching for David with the intent to kill. Instead of conquering the real enemies of Israel, he was driven by jealousy and anger to get rid of one who had served his people well. His downward journey took him from the presence of God into the house of a witch. Saul's life ended in disgrace.

Lying and suppressing the truth are serious matters.

Biblical History of Lying

Biblical history records over and over again the way in which lying compounds evil.

Now there was a famine in the land; so Abram went down to Egypt to sojourn there, for the famine was severe in the land. And it came about when he came near to Egypt, that he said to Sarai his wife, "See now, I know that you are a beautiful woman; and it will come about when the Egyptians see you, that they will say, 'This is his wife';

and they will kill me, but they will let you live. Please say that you are my sister so that it may go well with me because of you, and that I may live on account of you." And it came about when Abram came into Egypt, the Egyptians saw that the woman was very beautiful. And Pharaoh's officials saw her and praised her to Pharaoh; and the woman was taken into Pharaoh's house. Therefore he treated Abram well for her sake; and gave him sheep and oxen and donkeys and male and female servants and female donkeys and camels. But the LORD struck Pharaoh and his house with great plagues because of Sarai, Abram's wife. Then Pharaoh called Abram and said, "What is this you have done to me? Why did you not tell me that she was your wife? Why did you say, She is my sister, so that I took her for my wife? Now then, here is your wife, take her and go." And Pharaoh commanded his men concerning him; and they escorted him away, with his wife and all that belonged to him (Genesis 12:10–20 NASB).

Abram tried lying. There was a famine in the land where he lived, but there was food in Egypt. So he and his wife Sarai moved to survive. Then he thought of a potential problem. His beloved Sarai was so beautiful that the Egyptians would want to take her. She was so beautiful they would kill him to get her. Here was a simple answer to the problem: "Tell them you are my sister." That way they wouldn't kill him.

How well did it work? Sure enough, the Egyptians saw her beauty. Abram was right; they wanted her. However, it didn't work out the way Abram had planned. Because she was his sister, they nabbed her and took her to the king's palace.

Look at the consequences. Not only did Abram's lie not work, it brought diseases on the king and all the people of his house. In the end, Abram and Sarai were expelled from Egypt. Again, as grandma might say, "Lyin' don't pay."

Lying is deeply ingrained in the human heart. We may be tempted to think that if the first lie doesn't work, another one might. Abram should have learned his lesson in Egypt, but he did not. When Abram was 99 years old, the Lord appeared to him, and changed his name.

> And when Abram was ninety years old and nine, the LORD appeared to Abram, and said unto him, I am the Almighty God; walk before me, and be thou perfect. And I will make my covenant between me and thee, and will multiply thee exceedingly. And Abram fell on his face: and God talked with him, saying, As for me, behold, my covenant is with thee, and thou shalt be a father of many nations. Neither shall thy name any more be called Abram, but thy name shall be Abraham; for a father of many nations have I made thee. And I will make thee exceeding fruitful, and I will make nations of thee, and kings shall come out of thee. And I will establish my covenant between me and thee and thy seed after thee in

their generations for an everlasting covenant, to be a God unto thee, and to thy seed after thee. And I will give unto thee, and to thy seed after thee, the land wherein thou art a stranger, all the land of Canaan, for an everlasting possession; and I will be their God. And God said unto Abraham, Thou shalt keep my covenant therefore, thou, and thy seed after thee in their generations (Genesis 17:1-9).

God made a covenant with Abram that called for a name change. He is now Abraham, the man to whom God appeared. The Lord also promised Abraham that he and his wife would have a son. This was such a "far out" promise that Abraham's wife Sarah laughed about it.

Abraham was so close to God that he interceded with Him on behalf of Sodom. At Abraham's bidding, God assured him that if He found ten righteous people there, He would not destroy. Considering Abraham's closeness to God and his personal exchange with God about Sodom, we cannot imagine that Abraham would lie again and disappoint his God!

Some years later, Abraham moved to the land of Gerar. There he found himself in a predicament similar to the situation in Egypt. He still had a beautiful wife and was concerned about what might happen to her. He thought no one feared God in this place, and he was afraid someone would kill him to get Sarah. Again, he solved his dilemma by telling people that Sarah was his sister. This shaded information reached the king's palace and King Abimelech sent his servants to get this woman and bring her to him.

However, the king had an unexpected dream. God told him he would die, that the woman was married!

> Behold, thou are but a dead man, for the woman which thou hast taken; for she is a man's wife (Genesis 20:3).

Quickly the king explained that he was innocent. Abraham himself had said she was his sister. He didn't know he was doing anything wrong.

Again, there were consequences for Abraham's lie. The king's life was threatened. If he didn't give Sarah back, the king and all his family would die. The king gave Abraham silver to prove that he was innocent. But the innocent action of the king brought judgment anyway. All the women in Abimelech's house were unable to have children. However, through repentance and Abraham's prayer, this judgment was lifted. This all came about because Abraham lied.

Lying Is Passed On

Abraham's lying was passed on to his son Isaac. In Genesis 26:6-11, Isaac repeated the same lie as his father had done. Lying and deception were then passed on to Isaac's son Jacob. Jacob lied to his father and tricked his older brother Esau out of his blessing.[1]

The consequences of this lying were bitter. The lying split Isaac's family. It brought deep distress on the father, and the mother soon became weary with life, asking, "What good will my life do me?" It stirred up so deep an anger in Esau that he resolved to kill his brother.

Jacob left his family and went to live with his uncle Laban. There, Jacob was the victim of more deception. Laban promised his younger daughter for seven years labor. Then he deceived Jacob by giving him his older daughter instead. Jacob had to work seven more years for his beloved Rachel. Laban changed Jacob's wages ten times in six years.

Lying followed each generation. Jacob's sons lied to their father, insinuating that a wild animal had destroyed their younger brother, Joseph. The brothers carried this weight on their consciences until they repented and confessed before Joseph. Their lies brought deep agony and untold misery to the family.

Joseph was sold as a slave when he was 17 years old. The slave dealers sold him again to an Egyptian named Potiphar, an officer of Pharaoh. Joseph was a faithful servant to Potiphar. He served so well that Potiphar put Joseph in charge of everything he owned. This boy could be trusted.

Potiphar's wife desired Joseph. He was a handsome and well-built young man. She wanted him to come to bed with her. Joseph knew this was wrong; therefore, he refused.

And it came to pass after these things, that his master's wife cast her eyes upon Joseph; and she said, Lie with me. But he refused, and said unto his master's wife, Behold, my master wotteth (knows) not what is with me in the house, and he hath committed all that he hath to my hand; There is none greater in this house than I; neither

44

hath he kept back anything from me but thee, because thou art his wife: how then can I do this great wickedness, and sin against God? And it came to pass, as she spake to Joseph day by day, that he hearkened not unto her, to lie by her, or to be with her (Genesis 39:7–10).

Potiphar's wife would not take "no" for an answer. She kept on sweet-talking Joseph. Joseph refused, and even refused to spend time with her. She became persistent and grabbed him by his coat.

And it came to pass about this time, that Joseph went into the house to do his business; and there was none of the men of the house there within. And she caught him by his garment, saying, Lie with me: and he left his garment in her hand, and fled, and got him out (Genesis 39:11, 12).

Her sinful scheme failed. So she made up a lie and claimed Joseph tried to rape her. Potiphar was told the made-up story.

And it came to pass, when she saw that he had left his garment in her hand, and was fled forth, That she called unto the men of her house, and spake unto them, saying, See, he hath brought in an Hebrew unto us to mock us; he came in unto me to lie with me, and I cried with a loud voice: And it came to pass, when he heard that I lifted up my voice and cried, that he left his garment with me, and fled, and got him out. And she laid up his garment by her, until his lord came home. And she spake unto him according to these words, saying, The Hebrew servant, which thou hast brought unto us, came in unto me to mock me: And it came to pass, as I lifted up my voice and cried, that he left his garment with me, and fled out. And it came to pass, when his master heard the words of his wife, which she spake unto him, saying, After this manner did thy servant to me; that his wrath was kindled. And Joseph's master took him, and put him into the prison, a place where the king's prisoners were bound: and he was there in the prison (Genesis 39:13–20).

The consequences of lying? It sent innocent Joseph to prison, Potiphar lost his best servant, and Potiphar's wife gained absolutely nothing but a guilty conscience and a strained relationship with her husband. Liars are losers. And again, as Grandma might say, "Lyin' don't pay."

Many accounts of relationships in the Bible include consequences of lying. When God created Adam and Eve, they were sinless, living in a heavenly Paradise. God instructed them to enjoy everything but the fruit of one tree.

And the LORD God took the man, and put him into the garden of Eden to dress it and to keep it. And the LORD God commanded the man, saying, Of every tree of the garden thou mayest freely eat: But of the tree of the knowledge of good and evil, thou shalt not eat of it: for in the day that thou eatest thereof thou shalt surely die (Genesis 2:15-17).

Satan was subtle and deceiving. He first planted a question: Did God really say they shouldn't eat of that tree? Eve replied that they shouldn't eat it nor touch it, "lest ye die." Satan replied with the big lie, "Ye shall not surely die."[2] There you have it: an absolute lie that contradicts the omniscient God who created the universe and its living occupants. The first couple fell for the lie and ate the forbidden fruit.

Were there consequences? Words cannot adequately describe the consequences that followed even to this very day. They lost their Paradise home. They lost their spiritual innocence and their connection with God. Their spiritual fellowship went dead the day they disobeyed.

Because they followed the lie and the liar, they were driven out of Paradise into a world of sorrow. There the ground was affected by the lie, so that it brought forth thorns and thistles. In this cursed world man now toils and sweats to get his bread. Man is now constantly faced with the threat of death. After all the sorrow and toiling, death overtakes man, and he dies.

The sin virus of following the lie has infected all mankind. It has passed from generation to generation right into our time.

The Bible speaks clearly about this. When King David

thought about his own sinfulness, God gave him this insight:

> Behold, I was shapen in iniquity; and in sin did my mother conceive me (Psalm 51:5).

The consequences of the big lie affected David at the time of conception. So it is passed on to all people, so that the bitter consequences of the big lie live on today. The New Testament states the case clearly:

> As it is written, There is none righteous, no, not one: There is none that understandeth, there is none that seeketh after God. They are all gone out of the way, they are together become unprofitable; there is none that doeth good, no, not one (Romans 3:10-12). For all have sinned, and come short of the glory of God (Romans 3:23).

The Liar's Eternal Future

Those who willfully practice lies will be exposed and doomed. Those who do not truly repent will not "get by." Their eternal future is a serious matter. The Apostle John saw a most desolate future for liars. He explained and warned about that future in the book of Revelation.

> But the fearful, and unbelieving, and the abominable, and murderers, and whoremongers, and sorcerers, and idolaters, and all liars, shall have their part in the lake which burneth with fire and brimstone: which is the second death (Revelation 21:8).

John was shown the holy city of God. This city had no need of the sun or the moon to shine on it. The glory of God illumined it, and the Lamb was its lamp. Take careful note of those who will in no wise enter the glorious city:

> And there shall in no wise enter into it any thing that defileth, neither whatsoever worketh abomination, or maketh a lie: but they which are written in the Lamb's book of life (Revelation 21:27).

> Blessed are they that do his commandments, that they may have right to the tree of life, and may enter in through the gates into the city. For without are dogs, and sorcerers, and whoremongers, and murderers, and idolaters, and whosoever loveth and maketh a lie (Revelation 22:14, 15).

Unrepentant liars will be eternally separated from God. They will spend eternity with the devil and his other liars. My friend, that is not a laughing matter. Lying is a very serious sin.

Think about it. . . .

The big lie sent Jesus Christ to the cross to die a criminal's death. There He died to deliver us from the consequences of the lie.

> For God sent not his Son into the world to condemn the world; but that the world through him might be saved (John 3:17).

Questions for Discussion

1. Do the effects of lying pass on to the coming generations? Give some Biblical proofs for your answer.
2. What should we do when we realize we have told a lie? See 1 John 1:9; James 5:16; Proverbs 28:13? How might this help us to avoid lying in the future?
3. How does our view of lying affect those around us?
4. If we take a light-hearted view of lying, how will we look at other sins? What sins do we consider worse than lying? Proverbs 6:16-19; 12:22.
5. Why are people prone to lying?
6. Name some Biblical characters who suffered from the consequences of their lying. What were the consequences?

CHAPTER FOUR

The Source of Lies

WHERE DID LYING ORIGINATE? WHO ESTABLISHED it? Who is the founding father and president of lying?

One thing for certain, it is not God! The Bible declares, "it was impossible for God to lie."[1] The Apostle Paul's letter to Titus refers to the "hope of eternal life, which God, that cannot lie, promised before the world began" (Titus 1:2).

Furthermore, God came and dwelt among us in His Son Jesus, who said: "I am . . . the truth."[2]

Lying had to originate with someone other than God.

When I was born, I was given a name. From the day of my birth this name has been used to identify who I am. It appears on my driver's license, on my checkbook, on my phone bill, and in dozens of other places. When I meet people for the first time, we shake hands and exchange names. Why? To identify who we are.

I get lots of sales calls. Many of them start out about

the same way, "Good morning, Mr. Schrock, this is _____," and they give their name to identify who they are.

Jesus has told us whose name is "Father of Lies." It is the devil. Jesus explained:

> He was a murderer from the beginning, and abode not in the truth, because there is no truth in him. When he speaketh a lie, he speaketh for his own: for he is a liar, and the father of it (John 8:44).

Satan, the Father of Lies!

You are not a stranger to the father of lies. He knows you quite well. He concerns himself with what you think, say, and do. He tries to influence what you do with your time, the places you go, and with whom you associate. He keeps an eye on you like a cat waiting to pounce on a mouse. You are acquainted with his existence, but he has hidden his true self behind a false mask. He does not give you his true identity. The Bible teaches that you should not be ignorant of his devices. The devil lies about who he really is, where he originates, and where he is going.

The Liar's Origin

Heaven is a place of perfect order. "All but the deity were creatures created by a loving God."[3] Each of the heavenly creatures accepted its responsibility and respected the limits of its authority.

In the realm of heaven there served one angel who was

particularly "full of wisdom, and perfect in beauty." He was "the model of perfection." He also was "in the garden of God."[4] He once stood among those beams of glory that surrounded the eternal heavenly Father. He was reverent toward the Creator God, cheerfully obeyed His every command, and enjoyed a close tie to the Son of God. He possessed a brightness! He was "the shining one."[5] His name was Lucifer—"morning star, son of the dawn."[6]

The God of heaven gave His creatures the awesome gift of choice and the frightening power to choose.

Lucifer made a choice! He chose to think more of himself than of God. "He seemed to forget that he was the creature—not the creator."[7]

He was determined to place his throne above the throne of God. Love and adoration of God was replaced with envy, jealousy, and even hatred of God's Son. Lucifer demanded equality with God and His Son. Thus, he stood in bold defiance before the throne of God.

I will exalt my throne above the stars of God (Isaiah 14:13). . . . I will be like the Most High (Isaiah 14:14).

This brought conflict to the serenity of heaven. The created Lucifer fought to become equal or above the Creator. In the midst of the struggle, the Father expelled Lucifer and his followers.

Jesus said,

I beheld Satan as lightning fall from heaven (Luke 10:18).

It is commonly believed that Lucifer was created by God, was part of the angel host, that he was a prince of heaven, an archangel. Then, because of his pride, he was cast out of heaven and is now known as Satan—the devil. According to 1 Timothy 3:6, he fell into the judgment and condemnation of God.

Lucifer was not alone in his sin; a host of other angels fell with him. The Bible mentions "the angels which kept not their first estate, but left their own habitation" (Jude 6a) and are now awaiting the great judgment of Christ.

Peter reminds us that

> God spared not the angels that sinned, but cast them down to hell, and delivered them into chains of darkness, to be reserved unto judgment (2 Peter 2:4).

Lucifer and a host of angels fell from heaven because they sinned and rebelled against God. Perhaps what the Apostle John saw and described in Revelation was Lucifer's fall and influence on the other angels.

> His tail swept a third of the stars out of the sky and flung them to the earth (Revelation 12:4, NIV).

There is no salvation for Lucifer and the fallen angels. Their judgment is sealed as they wait for the great judgment of Christ. God revealed to John what is ahead for the devil and his demons.

> And the devil that deceived them was cast into the lake of fire and brimstone, where the beast

and false prophet are, and shall be tormented day and night for ever and ever . . . And death and hell were cast into the lake of fire. This is the second death. And whosoever was not found written in the book of life was cast into the lake of fire (Revelation 20:10, 14, 15).

Their destiny is sealed! Redemption is not offered to them. Heaven is now and forever closed to Satan and the fallen angels.

Now that Lucifer, the devil, is forever sealed out of heaven, he and his demons are waging a battle to take honor away from God the Creator. Because he cannot become equal with God, he is fighting to deny mankind the access to God that he himself once had. Because there is no salvation for him, he is fighting to keep you from having it and from glorifying God in your salvation. A condemned devil and his demons are on the warpath.

What Is the Liar Like?

Sometimes he, like a roaring lion, "walketh about, seeking whom he may devour."[8] He is the adversary of God and mankind. He takes an opposing, hostile position against God. He is an opponent of God and God's people. He is the slanderer of God and man. He slandered God to man when he said, "Hath God said?"[9] He slandered man to God when he asked, "Doth Job fear God for naught?"[10]

He is the destroyer, the dragon, the prince of this world. He is the god of this world, "the prince of the power of the air." He is "the spirit that now worketh in the children of disobedience." He is the constant enemy of God, of Christ, and of His divine kingdom. He is the enemy of the followers of Christ.

He excites and induces evil in every possible way. He is the power of darkness, the sower of tares in your life. He is a serpent, a wolf, a lion. Pretending to be a messenger of light, he is the enemy of truth. To make his lies believable, he "disguises himself as an angel of light."[11] He is afraid of the truth. He cannot be truthful about who he is and what his goals are. He is full of falsehood and malice.

Satan is the one who brought "the big lie" to the human race. God created man and woman in His own image. When he placed them in the Garden of Eden, they had only one restriction, as a means of showing love and worship to their Creator. They were not to eat the fruit of one certain tree. Life would be a Paradise as long as they obeyed God. But Satan came to them with "the lie."

He still lies to people about their need of salvation. He is the one who makes people believe they do not need the blood of Jesus Christ to take away their sins. He is the one who tells people to neglect salvation and not take the church too seriously.

> In whose case the god of this world has blinded the minds of the unbelieving, that they might not see the light of the gospel of the glory of Christ, who is the image of God (2 Corinthians 4:4, NASB).

Jesus put it straight: "He is a liar, and the father of it" (John 8:44).

The lying of this world comes from the devil. The lying people in our lying culture are following the ways of the devil. The problem of lying that plagues us comes from people who allow the devil to convince them to become liars.

Would you want to buy a used car from a known liar? Would you take your car to a garage that is known for dishonesty and cheating? Would you trust making any kind of deal with a known crook? Probably not! And you would pass the word around: "Don't take your car to that crook."

The devil is the liar! He is the enemy of truth. Why would you even think of listening to any of his lies? A crook is not a good person to work on your car. Neither is the devil a trustworthy person in any area of your life. Liars are influenced by the devil and are assisting his cause. My friend, that makes lying a very serious matter.

Now the serpent was more subtil than any beast of the field which the LORD God had made. And he said unto the woman, Yea, hath God said, Ye shall not eat of every tree of the garden? And the woman said unto the serpent, We may eat of the fruit of the trees of the garden: But of the fruit of the tree which is in the midst of the garden, God hath said, Ye shall not eat of it, neither shall ye touch it, lest ye die. And the serpent said unto the woman, Ye shall not surely die: For God doth know that in the day ye eat thereof, then your eyes shall be opened, and ye shall be as gods, knowing good and evil (Genesis 3:1-5).

Satan contradicted God. The big lie was that they would not die if they ate of the forbidden fruit. They followed Satan's lie and ate. Their heavenly relationship with God died and God cast them out of Eden. They lived the rest of their life under the dark shadow of Satan's lie. Mankind has been bound, blinded, and held captive by the big lie ever since, and that is not something to laugh about!

1. Hebrews 6:18.
2. John 14:6.
3. Moore, Raymond S., *The Adaddon Conspiracy*, Bethany House, 1985, p. 12.
4. Ezekiel 28:12, 13.
5. Meredith, J. L., *Meredith's Book of Lists*, Bethany House, 1980, p. 239.
6. Isaiah 14:12, NIV.
7. Moore, Raymond S., *The Adaddon Conspiracy*, Bethany House, 1985, p.13.
8. 1 Peter 5:8.
9. Genesis 3:1.
10. Job 1:9.
11. 2 Corinthians 11:14, NASB.

Questions for Discussion

1. Before his expulsion from heaven, what did Lucifer begin to desire? Can we relate to being possessed by a selfish agenda?
2. What is Satan's destiny?
3. How much can we deviate from truth before we become pawns in the hands of the deceiver?
4. Why are things just beyond our grasp or things denied us so attractive (as the tree of the knowledge of good and evil was to Adam and Eve)?
5. How often have you consciously or unconsciously entertained the devil's question: "Yea, hath God said?"
6. How much untruth is required before the whole statement is distorted?
7. How can a deceived person ever recognize his or her state of deception?
8. Which of Satan's names tells us about his untruthfulness?

CHAPTER FIVE

Whom Can You Trust?

SINCE THE DEVIL IS *THE* LIAR AND THE FATHER OF LIES, where does truth exist? We know we live in a lying culture where the big question is "Whom can you trust?"

A person known for lying cannot be counted on to speak words of truth. I would be skeptical about buying a used car from a known liar.

Jesus Christ was led to Pilate's hall of judgment. There Pilate asked the famous question, "What is truth?"[1] "What is truth?" and "Whom can you trust?" are still very relevant questions. These questions need to be answered in the very depth of our soul and spirit.

Was there ever a human being who embodied truth? Was there ever anyone who could be depended on to be always truthful? Where can a person go to find established truth? How about the dictionary? Of course not, it is constantly changing. How about the *World Book Encyclopedia*? It is right sometimes and wrong sometimes. What about the best educators? Many never arrive at a final truth. They are "ever learning, and never able to come to the knowledge of the truth."[2]

The book that exposes the devil and declares him to be the father of lies also introduces us to the One who is truth: Christ, who is revealed in the Bible.

Truth Came to Moses

Moses was miraculously saved from the wrath of Pharaoh. The king of Egypt ordered that "every son that is born, ye shall cast into the river" (Exodus 1:22). When Moses was born, his mother made a basket that floated like a boat. She put him in it and took it to the edge of the Nile River where she left it in the tall grass. The king's daughter found the basket and the crying baby in it. Her heart melted with compassion toward this cute little Hebrew baby. Pharaoh's daughter arranged for and paid a nurse to take care of the treasure she found. The nurse she paid to care for Moses was his own mother.

When Moses was a grown man, God appeared to him in a miraculous way. God called to Moses "out of the midst" of a burning bush. There God called Moses to deliver the children of Israel from the bondage of Egypt and Pharaoh. God introduced himself to Moses as **"I AM THAT I AM."**

> And God said to Moses, **I AM WHO I AM**, and **WHAT I AM** and **I WILL BE WHAT I WILL BE** (Exodus 3:14, *Amplified Bible*).

God had a special relationship with Moses. The Bible says,

> And the LORD spake unto Moses face to face, as a man speaketh unto his friend (Exodus 33:11).

After Moses led Israel out of Egypt, God called him to come up onto Mount Sinai. There God gave Moses the Ten Commandments. While Moses was up in the mountain, the people he led out of Egypt turned to idolatry. When Moses saw the golden calf and the dancing of the people, he became angry and threw the tablets of stone out of his hands and broke them. Later, God called Moses to bring another set of stones to Mt. Sinai. There God Himself would write the words that were on the first set. Moses cut two stone tablets like the first ones and met God. Something significant happened there. Notice what God proclaimed to Moses:

> And the LORD descended in the cloud, and stood with him there, and proclaimed the name of the LORD. And the LORD passed by before him, and proclaimed, The LORD, The LORD God, merciful and gracious, longsuffering, and abundant in goodness and truth (Exodus 34:5, 6).

God presented himself to Moses as "abundant in truth." Some translations use the word "faithfulness" instead of "truth." God presented himself—"abounding in love and faithfulness" (NIV). Does the change of words change the meaning? Faithfulness means "accurate; true to the facts."[3]

Put the two translations together, and we have God presenting himself to Moses as the person who is abundant in truth, accurate, and true to the facts. Moses was learning that God is the source of truth. God is faithful to His Word. God's Word can be trusted.

Moses' life was a long walk with God. As he approached the end of his life, he wrote a song of praise to God to leave with his people. It is known as the Song of Moses. In this song he gives honor to God. Notice what he ascribes to God:

> He is the Rock, his work is perfect: for all his ways are judgment: a God of truth and without iniquity, just and right is he (Deuteronomy 32:4).
>
> A God of faithfulness and without injustice (NASB).

After Moses' long and personal experience with God, he proclaimed Him to be the "God of truth" and the "God of faithfulness."

Where can we find truth? What is truth? Who can we trust? As Moses declared, it is God.

The human race had been living under the influence of the lie in Eden. The devil brought the lie to our first parents. They yielded to it, and people have been walking in the dark shadow of the lie ever since. Now God revealed Himself to Moses as the God of truth.

Truth Came to David

David was a man whose heart was after God. He experienced and maintained a spiritual relationship with God. He expressed confidence in God as he wrote many Psalms. He, too, realized there was truth and God was that truth.

Into thine hand I commit my spirit: thou hast redeemed me, O Lord God of truth (Psalm 31:5).

In another Psalm David wrote:

I will praise thee, O Lord, among the people: I will sing unto thee among the nations. For thy mercy is great unto the heavens, and thy truth unto the clouds. Be thou exalted, O God, above the heavens: let thy glory be above all the earth (Psalm 57:9-11).

David's experience with God moved him to write about the God of truth. David saw the light of truth shining past the big lie. David believed God was true and trustworthy.

Who is truth and whom can you trust? The Psalms declare that it is God.

For the Lord is good; his mercy is everlasting; and his truth endureth to all generations (Psalm 100:5).

And the truth of the Lord endureth for ever (Psalm 117:2).

Thy law is the truth (Psalm 119:142).

And all thy commandments are truth (Psalm 119:151).

Truth Came to Isaiah

The prophet Isaiah was moved in heart to give praise to God. Isaiah, too, got a glimpse of who is true, faithful, and trustworthy. He expressed his praise in this Scripture:

O LORD, thou art my God; I will exalt thee, I will praise thy name; for thou hast done wonderful things; thy counsels of old are faithfulness and truth (Isaiah 25:1).

Isaiah saw past the big lie and beheld the wonderful, faithful God of truth.

Truth Came to Daniel

Daniel was shown a vision. In that vision, he saw a man dressed in linen. His face was bright like lightning, his eyes like fire. His arms and legs were shiny like polished brass. His voice sounded like the roar of a crowd. Daniel was frightened, lost his strength, and turned white like a dead person. He was helpless. Then one who looked like a man touched Daniel

And said, O man greatly beloved, fear not: peace be unto thee, be strong, yea, be strong (Daniel 10:19).

The man delivered this message to Daniel:

But I will show thee that which is noted in the scripture of truth (Daniel 10:21).

But before I go, I must first tell you what is written in the book of Truth (Daniel 10:21, NCV).

Is there such a thing as truth, something trustworthy? Rest assured, truth exists. Daniel was told of the "scripture of truth." Daniel did not have to live in darkness, blinded by the big lie the devil told in Eden.

Is There Someone We Can Trust?

So there is a "God of truth" and a "scripture of truth." But is there not some human being we can trust? Is there not a source of truth somewhere in a living body? The Bible says, "There is none righteous, no, not one" (Romans 3:10).

That means finding a person among humans who is "truth" is hopeless. There is no person who can shine through the big lie of Eden in their own strength.

God does not want us to walk in darkness and under the shadow of the lie. He promised to give a light to those who sit in darkness and to guide our feet into the way of peace.

The people that walked in darkness have seen a great light: they that dwell in the land of the shadow of death, upon them hath the light shined (Isaiah 9:2).

To give light to them that sit in darkness and in

the shadow of death, to guide our feet into the way of peace (Luke 1:79).

The good news—the exciting news—is that God knew there was no human being who could become "the truth"; therefore, He sent His Son out of heaven's glory to become a human being and be that person who is Truth.

God sent His Son from heaven into the womb of a woman to be born a baby, just as we were. As John wrote:

> And the Word was made flesh, and dwelt among us, (and we beheld his glory, the glory as of the only begotten of the Father,) full of grace and truth (John 1:14).

> For the law was given by Moses, but grace and truth came by Jesus Christ (John 1:17).

Jesus Christ became the truth in a human person. He came here and lived among us. He came to preach the gospel to the poor, to heal the brokenhearted, and to preach deliverance to those who are held captive by the big lie of the devil (see Luke 4:18). He came to give liberty from Satan's deception. He came to pay the price to deliver you from the power of darkness and to transform you into the kingdom of his dear Son.[4]

Jesus Christ came to be the truth in person, in order to deliver you from the grips of the liar and the lie, and to put you into the peaceful arms of truth. The big lie in Eden was delivered by a serpent. That serpent received a curse and became an ugly snake. Snakes symbolize the bondage of the big lie. Some are deadly, poisonous. One bite and the victim perishes. Some snakes are long and strong. They can coil themselves around a person, squeezing the person tightly to death.

The human race is poisoned and captured by the devil's lie. Jesus Christ, the truth, came to set us free. He said:

> Ye shall know the truth, and the truth shall make you free (John 8:32).

What dispels a lie? The truth!

The farmer gives his boy a bag of bean seed with instructions on how to plant them. Plant them beside the row of corn about three inches apart. Push them into the fine ground with your finger. Soon the boy is back. "It's all done, Dad."

"How can you be done so soon? Did you plant them as I instructed you?"

"Yes, Dad!"

About a week later the truth comes up. Beans by the handful are sprouting thickly in several places where the seeds were buried in bunches. The truth dispels the lie.

Where can you turn to find the truth? Is there anyone you can trust? Truth is here—truth is among us. It is in the person Jesus Christ. Do not let the lie disturb your peace.

> Let not your heart be troubled: ye believe in God, believe also in me. In my Father's house are many mansions: if it were not so, I would have told you.

I go to prepare a place for you. And if I go and prepare a place for you, I will come again, and receive you unto myself; that where I am, there ye may be also. And whither I go ye know, and the way ye know. Thomas saith unto him, Lord, we know not whither thou goest; and how can we know the way? Jesus saith unto him, I am the way, the truth, and the life: no man cometh unto the Father, but by me (John 14:1-6).

Who is the truth? Jesus Christ. Jesus Christ can release us from the bondage of the lie and the liar. He gave His life to redeem us from the cruse of the lie. His body was taken from the cross and buried. But the grave could not hold Him. He arose and is alive forevermore, and His truth lives on today. This truth shall set you free.

Jesus said, "No man cometh unto the Father, but by me." Why is Jesus the only way? Because He is the only person who is Truth, and only His truth can dispel the devil's lie. He Himself is the truth that can set you free from Satan's coil of bondage.

True Christians are those who realize that they were spiritually lost, captivated by the lie. They are the ones who have come to the truth and have been set free. In them the Spirit of truth dwells, because Jesus, the Truth, sends His Spirit, the Spirit of truth, to live in His true followers. We can be persons of truth!

The fact that Christ's followers can have the Spirit of truth living in them is precisely what makes lying such a serious offense against God.

I remember the picture of President Clinton coming out of church with his big Bible in hand. Now we know that he had lied a short time earlier. God is sinfully disgraced when someone professes to have the Spirit of truth living within them but utters words that come from the spirit of the devil, the liar, the father of lies.

Is there anyone who can be trusted? Does truth exist in anyone? Yes! Jesus Christ is truth. He can be trusted. That is good news for those who want to be persons of truth but live in a culture of lying. Truth is alive and can be present in our lives.

---

1. John 18:38.
2. 2 Timothy 3:7.
3. "Faithfulness," *The Complete Christian Dictionary for Home and School,* Gospel Light, 1992.
4. See Galatians 1:13.

Questions for Discussion

1. Who can we trust?
2. Where can truth be found in today's world?
3. Who is the source of all truth?
4. Why is lying such a serious offense?
5. Who brings the truth into followers of Christ?
6. How did God present Himself to Moses?

CHAPTER SIX

Liars Can Change

CAN PEOPLE WHO PRACTICE LYING CHANGE? DO LIARS always have to be liars? What can be done to change the epidemic of lying that is commonplace in our culture? Should we make more laws to deal with it? Should people be required to swear to tell the truth?

Human effort will not change the heart of a liar. Lawmakers constantly make new laws to make it harder to get by with dishonesty. But people go on lying. Somewhere beyond rules and laws, there is a way for liars actually to become truthful people of integrity.

We can take a lesson from wicked King Ahab, who ruled Israel for 22 years. Ahab did more evil in God's sight than any of the kings before him. He did more things to make God angry than any of his predecessors. We read about Ahab in 1 Kings 16:24–22:40.

God warned King Ahab many times and gave him several opportunities to turn to God. God demonstrated His power through Elijah at the Mt. Carmel contest, when fire came from heaven and consumed Elijah's sacrifice and the water he had poured upon it. The false prophets of Baal were killed.

Soon after this great demonstration of God's power, King Ahab coveted a vineyard near his palace. The garden belonged to a common man named Naboth. It was Naboth's inheritance, and he wanted to keep it that way. Therefore, in spite of Ahab's pleading, Naboth would not sell the vineyard to the king.

King Ahab went home angry and upset and lay down on his bed and pouted. He turned his face toward the wall and refused to eat.

Ahab's wife Jezebel was a chief promoter of evil. She continually encouraged Ahab to sin. Jezebel took the matter of the vineyard in her own hands, saying, "I will get the vineyard for you." She fabricated a lie about Naboth. She wrote letters in King Ahab's name and sealed them with the official, royal seal. The letters were sent to the elders and rulers of Naboth's city. They falsely charged Naboth with blaspheming God and the king. Jezebel pulled off a quick, phony trial, had Naboth declared guilty, and then stoned to death. "Here, King Ahab, is your vineyard!" And off went the king to take possession.

However, while Jezebel was giving Ahab the news of his vineyard, God was sending verdicts of judgment: God will bring evil upon you. Your family will be completely destroyed. The dogs and the birds will eat the dead bodies of your family. The dogs that licked up Naboth's blood will lick up your blood in the same place.

When this wicked king coveted his neighbor's goods

and his wicked wife secured a false conviction against an innocent man, God's anger was stirred and judgment was pronounced.

But something happened to Ahab. When he received the message of judgment, he saw his sinfulness before God. He humbled himself, tore his clothes, and put on sackcloth. He fasted and went around quietly and meekly. This exceedingly wicked King Ahab acknowledged his sin.

The Lord who saw the wickedness of King Ahab now saw his humility. The Lord spoke to His prophet Elijah,

> Seest thou how Ahab humbleth himself before me? Because he humbleth himself before me, I will not bring the evil in his days: but in his son's days will I bring the evil upon his house (1 Kings 21:29).

This account gives us a look into God's view of lying. You know how disgusting it is when you know someone is lying to you. Jezebel's lies about Naboth stirred up God's wrath and His judgment. Whereas lying is disgusting to honest people, it is evil and sinful in the sight of God. It carries with it bitter consequences.

For this reason, liars need an Ahab experience. They need to see how sinful lying is in God's eyes. As Ahab saw his wickedness and humbled himself before God, so liars need to see their wickedness as God sees it. They need to humble themselves in true repentance before God. An Ahab-like humility and repentance can be the start of a dramatic change in any person's life. It is the right move toward changing.

God promised His people Israel that if they would humble themselves and seek His forgiveness, He would forgive them.

> If my people, which are called by my name, shall humble themselves, and pray, and seek my face, and turn from their wicked ways; then will I hear from heaven, and will forgive their sin, and will heal their land (2 Chronicles 7:14).

Here is my paraphrase of this promise for liars: If liars shall humble themselves, and pray, and seek my face, and turn from their wicked lying, I will forgive them and bring healing to their lives.

Repentance and humility take a person beyond New Year's resolutions and superficial ideas about minor changes. Humility is necessary for true repentance to occur. And repentance must invite the Spirit of Truth to enter the heart. Lies and lying come from the spirit of the devil. Truth and truthfulness come from Jesus Christ and His Holy Spirit of Truth.

The spirit that has chief residence in the heart is the spirit that controls the life. You cannot be a truthful person if the spirit of the liar is the chief resident of your heart. You cannot be truthful if you are in bondage to serving the father of lies. To be a truthful person, you must give the Spirit of Truth chief residence in your heart.

Oswald Chambers, in *My Utmost for His Highest,* said this:

> We have to recognize that sin is a fact. Either God

or sin must die in my life. The New Testament brings us right down to this one issue. If sin rules in me, God's life in me will be killed; if God rules in me, sin in me will be killed.[1]

When the Spirit of Truth, Jesus Christ, is given chief residence in the heart, then sin must die. Lying must die before freedom from sin can come.

As Jesus said,

And ye shall know the truth, and the truth shall make you free (John 8:32).

The Spirit of Truth makes a person free from dishonesty and lying. "The truth God wants us to know is really the truth with a capital T."[2] Jesus Christ is the Truth.

A Pharisee named Nicodemus came to Jesus one night with some critical questions. Jesus gave him some life-changing answers. Jesus told Nicodemus:

Except a man be born again, he cannot see the kingdom of God (John 3:3).

Puzzled, Nicodemus asked:

How can a man be born when he is old? can he enter the second time into his mother's womb, and be born? (John 3:4).

This did not make sense to Nicodemus, so Jesus explained further:

That which is born of the flesh is flesh; and that which is born of the Spirit is spirit. Marvel not that I said unto thee, Ye must be born again (John 3:6, 7).

Jesus explained to Nicodemus that a person's body is born from human parents. However, a person's spiritual life is born from the Spirit.

In this dialogue, Jesus presented the gospel in a nutshell. This is recorded in the much quoted John 3:16.

For God so loved the world, that he gave his only begotten Son, that whosoever believeth in him should not perish, but have everlasting life.

Here is good news for liars and all other sinners. They can change. They can humble themselves, recognize their lostness and need of the Savior, seek God's forgiveness, believe on the Lord Jesus Christ and His work of atonement, and be saved. Here is the invitation to open the door of your heart to Christ and yield your spirit to give him full residence.

As we used to sing in summer Bible school:

Into my heart, into my heart,
Come into my heart, Lord Jesus.
Come in today, come in to stay;
Come into my heart, Lord Jesus.

When the Spirit of Truth, the Spirit of the living God, takes up residence in your heart (your spirit), you are born again. Your spiritual life is born from God's Spirit.

Born again people can live above sin. They can be released and set free from lying. The Spirit of God who lives in them is greater than the spirit of evil that is in the world. The Spirit of Truth can overpower and overcome the spirit of lies. The Bible says:

> Ye are of God, little children, and have overcome them: because greater is he that is in you, than he that is in the world (1 John 4:4).

After being born of the Spirit, the new Christian experiences the growing process. As a newborn baby needs to feed and grow, so the spiritual newborn needs to feed on the Word of God and grow in the grace and knowledge of Jesus Christ. The new life needs to keep coming in, and the old needs to go out. The Bible calls the believer to lay aside and put away old patterns of living.

> Wherefore laying aside all malice, and all guile, and hypocrisies, and envies, and all evil speakings, As newborn babes, desire the sincere milk of the word, that ye may grow thereby (1 Peter 2:1, 2).

> Wherefore putting away lying, speak every man truth with his neighbor: for we are members one of another (Ephesians 4:25).

Believers are to constantly keep on conforming to the image of Christ. They are to put on the mind of Christ and develop thinking as Jesus Christ thinks. Believers should be putting away lying. Does all this come at once? No, it is a growing process. That is why the Bible calls for born again people to "grow in grace, and in the knowledge of our Lord and Savior Jesus Christ" (2 Peter 3:18).

A Formula for Growth

The Bible gives the believer a growth formula. It is God's will that His people be thoroughly and adequately equipped for every good work. God wants His people to be equipped to live honestly. He wants them to be free from lying.

Believers are vulnerable. Each of us has areas of greater temptation, things that are very difficult for us to "put away." New believers are not fully aware of the will of God in every area of the Christian life. Some new believers may think lying is not such a serious offense. After all, "everybody does it." This is why we need to know the Word of God.

The Apostle Paul wrote instructions, under the inspiration of God, to a young man named Timothy. In Paul's letter he explained that in the latter days perilous and difficult times will come. Included in the list of sinners prevalent in the last days are false accusers and slanderers who will flaunt "a form of godliness, but [deny] the power thereof."[3] These people will have a form of religion but not the overcoming power to live lives that honor and please God. They may be seen coming out of church with their Bibles, but they will not have the power of the Spirit of Truth to deliver them from lying.

Paul's letter to Timothy urges all believers to become thoroughly equipped to do all good works. This includes "putting away lying and speaking truth with your neighbor." One problem new believers face is that many who call themselves Christians are still trapped by the father of lies.

> But evil men and seducers shall wax worse and worse, deceiving, and being deceived. But continue thou in the things which thou hast learned and hast been assured of, knowing of whom thou hast learned them; And that from a child thou hast known the holy scriptures, which are able to make thee wise unto salvation through faith which is in Christ Jesus. All scripture is given by inspiration of God, and is profitable for doctrine, for reproof, for correction, for instruction in righteousness: That the man of God may be perfect, thoroughly furnished unto all good works (2 Timothy 3:13-17).

Evil people are going from bad to worse, and they continue to deceive and be deceived. But we are told to continue in the things that we have learned and are "assured of." In this we find God's formula for growing, becoming like Jesus, and putting on the mind of Christ. After the reference to salvation, the new birth experience, and the entrance of God's Spirit, we are given five important principles, a formula for changing and being made over into the likeness of Jesus Christ. This is the kind of change that fully equips us for all good works.

Here are the five principles:

1. All Scripture is given by the inspiration of God, and is profitable
2. Profitable for doctrine

3. Profitable for reproof
4. Profitable for correction
5. Profitable for instruction in righteousness

How can these principles bring change in the life of a person who lies or commits any other sin that prevents him from being fully equipped in all good works?

First Step. For the truth to set you free, you must believe that the Word of God is truth. You must believe that all Scripture is given by the inspiration of God and is profitable for today and applies to people today. You must believe that God's word is truth.[4]

Second Step. Not only must you believe the Word, but you also must learn and teach the Word. The Scripture is profitable for doctrine. A step toward change is opening yourself to sound doctrine. Doctrine means instruction and teaching. To be thoroughly equipped for all good works, you must be instructed in the Word and will of God.

As the Bible says,

Study to shew thyself approved unto God, a workman that needeth not to be ashamed, rightly dividing the word of truth (2 Timothy 2:15).

You need to be instructed in the Word because

The word of God is quick, and powerful, and sharper than any twoedged sword, piercing even to the dividing asunder of soul and spirit, and of the joints and marrow, and is a discerner of the thoughts and intents of the heart (Hebrews 4:12).

To change, you need to know the Word. You need to be clearly reminded that God hates "a lying tongue" and that the following are an abomination to Him:

A proud look, a lying tongue, and hands that shed innocent blood (Proverbs 6:17).

You need to be reminded from the inspired Word of God that the Word calls you to put away lying and speak the truth to every man.

What this means in practical terms is that you need to read the Bible over and over from cover to cover. It also means that you need to take advantage of Bible study, preaching, and discussions of God's Word.

Third Step.   As you read the Word, you must also be open to reproof. Reproof means conviction as in criticism for a fault. Remember, the Spirit of Truth has taken up residence in the believer.

Jesus said:

Howbeit when he, the Spirit of truth, is come, he will guide you into all truth: for he shall not speak of himself; but whatsoever he shall hear, that shall he speak: and he will show you things to come (John 16:13).

As you read the Word, be open for the Spirit to bring conviction. If you are not fully honest, the Spirit may bring conviction as you read the Word.

As you are reminded that God hates "a lying tongue," the Spirit will bring to your remembrance that you lied to the insurance company and collected an extra $700. Or the Spirit may remind you that you lied to your wife about coming home three hours late, or perhaps that you falsely claimed an extra $1000 deduction on your 1040—or any of the things you have lied about.

Fourth Step. When the Spirit brings conviction, make corrections. When corrections are made, peace with God will come. Come humbly before God as King Ahab did. Then to make correction truly, get up from your knees and get your checkbook and stationery.

Dear IRS:

On my return dated_____, I deliberately lied and cheated on my deductions. According to my calculations I still owe_____ plus penalties and late fees. I'm truly sorry about this. God's Word has convicted me that it was wrong.

Fifth Step. Every believer needs "instruction in righteousness." This means disciplined training in righteousness. The Christian life is not a constant, happy-go-lucky experience as you flow downstream with the current. It is traveling upstream fighting the good fight of faith. Every believer has his or her own harder-to-conquer areas. Those are the areas that needs "disciplined training." The addicted liar may not find total release from the habit through confession alone. The person addicted to lying may need to call for help. Lying may have become a habit, a groove so deep that the victim may need someone to help. Many believers find help and victory over such deep-seated sin by becoming accountable to another believer. This person keeps in contact with the one needing help, who agrees to be open and honest about the progress being made.

Sometimes counseling with a pastor or other mature believer is helpful in changing stubborn habits. The good news is that even the deep-rooted sins that beset us can be overcome. Being honest before God and your brothers and sisters will allow you to know the truth, and the truth shall set you free.

Can liars change? Indeed they can. The Spirit of Truth is ready to make revolutionary changes in your spirit. The Word of God is available to bring conviction. There are brothers and sisters in God's family willing to stand with you through disciplined training in righteousness.

God bless you as you walk in the Truth.

1. Chambers, Oswald, *My Utmost of His Highest*, Barlow and Company Edition, 1935, p. 175.
2. Pritchard, Ray, *Names of the Holy Spirit,* Moody Press, 1995, p. 205.
3. 2 Timothy 3:5.
4. John 17:17.

God wants His children
on the top step of the ladder

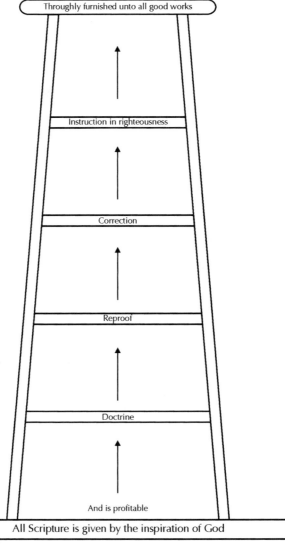

Throughly furnished unto all good works

Instruction in righteousness

Correction

Reproof

Doctrine

And is profitable

All Scripture is given by the inspiration of God

Steps up the ladder of changing
"unto all good works"

Questions for Discussion

1. What happened to the false prophets of Baal?
2. How did God respond to Ahab's humility and repentance?
3. How does God see lying?
4. To be a truthful person, what must we make the chief resident in our hearts?
5. What is the good news for all liars and other sinners?
6. What makes it possible for born again people to live above lying and sin?
7. What two things can the Spirit of Truth do to the spirit of lies?
8. What must we believe and know to be thoroughly equipped to all good works?
9. What is "reproof"?
10. Who guides us into all truth and brings conviction of sin?
11. Do you believe that liars can change? Explain your answer in your own words and discuss it with others in your study group.
12. In what areas of your life would you most likely be tempted to lie to avoid embarrassment, punishment or payment?

CHAPTER SEVEN

Honesty Delights God

MY WIFE, OUR SON IVAN, AND I CAME HOME FROM church on a hot summer Sunday when the temperature was 94 degrees. Because the weather forecast had predicted it would be very hot that day, my son's dog was permitted to stay in the house while we were at church. The dog's name is Biscuit. His mother was a boxer and his father a community hound. This combination produced a big dog with a touch of friendliness. Usually when we come home, Biscuit greets us with welcome gestures from his entire body. He wiggles and wags all over with excitement at seeing us come home. This particular Sunday we got no welcome wiggles or wags. He didn't even come to the door.

Biscuit likes to raid trash cans for scraps of food, but Ivan has told him very sternly that's a no-no. In fact, Biscuit has gotten numerous rounds of discipline for violation of that rule.

This particular Sunday, Biscuit lay behind the table

simply shaking with regret and dog sorrow. There was trash all over the floor. He was a bad dog while we were gone!

Biscuit knows better. He knows there is trouble on the way if the trash is on the floor when his master comes home. While he knows better, he doesn't have the inner power to resist the smell of ham scraps when he is left alone. God did not provide for dogs to receive the Spirit of Truth into their spirit. Dogs are not given the power of the Holy Spirit to resist temptation. Therefore, Biscuit's dog nature takes control when he smells ham in the trash can or sees a rabbit across the street. Life for Biscuit and his master would have been much better if Biscuit would have eaten his dog food and left the trash in the can.

God created humans in His image, and He promised that those created in His image could have the new nature of truth. This is provided for us by Jesus Christ. Unlike Biscuit, we have power available to us to overcome temptation. We can live above our sin nature. We can be victorious over lying or any other sin. God's Spirit is available to give us that overcoming strength.

The Bible contains a list of sins that includes cheating, which is a form of lying. It explains that those who practice these sins shall not inherit the kingdom of God. Then it says,

> And such were some of you: but ye are washed, but ye are sanctified, but ye are justified in the name of the Lord Jesus, and by the Spirit of our God (1 Corinthians 6:11).

God's Spirit in the believer provides overcoming power to live above dishonesty. God's Spirit, who brings the convicting power of His Word, makes us persons of truth. That's a benefit Biscuit doesn't have.

The job of the police is to stop drivers who drive in an unsafe manner. Often such drivers are intoxicated. That's what country folks call "drunk." In many states, such a driver will be charged with DUI—driving under the influence. A DUI driver is dangerous to other people on the road; alcohol influences their actions and judgments.

The born again Christian can be under the influence of the Holy Spirit. That makes the believer an LUI. Ray Pritchard wrote, "Perhaps we should pray to be found LUI—Living Under the Influence of the Holy Spirit."[1] Indeed, the believer can be LUI. The Bible makes that point clear:

> But he who practices truth—who does what is right—comes out into the light; so that his works may be plainly shown to be what they are, wrought with God—divinely prompted, done with God's help, in dependence upon him (John 3:21, *Amplified Bible*).

With God's help, His people become outstanding people of truth and integrity. They have the power to stay out of the "trash can" of lying. Their sin need not be scattered on the floor of their lives. Something unique happens when God's children deliberately practice truth and honesty. The Bible says,

Who may ascend into the hill of the LORD?
And who may stand in His holy place?
He who has clean hands and a pure heart,
Who has not lifted up his soul to falsehood,
And has not sworn deceitfully.
He shall receive a blessing from the LORD
And righteousness from the God of his salvation
(Psalm 24:3-5, NASB).

These verses not only tell us that God is watching,[2] they also make clear that God allows the honest person to come into His presence without fear. The one who puts away lying will be accepted by God. Furthermore, God promises to bless that person with the gift of righteousness from God! What a wonderful promise! What a powerful motivation to pursue truthfulness.

When Honesty Is the Rule

We have looked at how God hates lying and dishonesty. We have seen that the Bible teaches us to put away lying and to be truthful. Yet, many people appear comfortable with what they call "a little white lie." God wants us to be honest in our dealings.

What happens when honesty is the rule for your life? The Bible tells us that it brings delight to God.

A false balance is abomination to the LORD; but a just weight is his delight (Proverbs 11:1).

Lying lips are abomination to the Lord: but they that deal truly are his delight (Proverbs 12:22).

God delights in seeing honesty practiced.

Menno Beachy, director of the Mountain Anthems Chorus for many years, has written his life story in a book entitled *Grace Enough for My Life's Journey*. It contains the account of his father leaving home when Menno was a little boy. His mother had to go to work to support her four children. She kept assuring them, "Yes, Dad will come back someday."

Menno stayed with his grandparents, who had planned to retire. Instead of retiring, they inherited four grandchildren ranging in age from four weeks to five years.

Menno writes about his godly grandfather and mentions a learning experience with his grandfather. "Grandpa was an honest and upright man," the book recounts. Grandpa purchased wheat from his son-in-law to feed his chickens. There was the kind of trust between the two men that allowed Grandpa to sack his own wheat. Menno helped his grandfather, probably holding the sack as Grandpa poured in the wheat.

Now take special notice to what happened as Grandpa and his little grandson measured the grain and poured it into the feedsack. Menno wrote, "I watched him level the half bushel measure with a board instead of rounding it full. He was not aware of the lesson of honesty that was coming through."[3]

So what? That was just a little incident in life. It would not have hurt to round it off a little. Right?

Get the picture here. Grandpa and his little grandson

are sacking wheat. Little Menno's inquisitive eyes watch as Grandpa levels off the wheat. According to Proverbs 15:3, the eyes of the Lord are watching too. As the eyes of the Lord look on, God is delighted. "A just weight is his delight."

What Grandpa and Menno didn't realize was that right there by the grain bin on a farm in western Maryland a worship of God was taking place. God was delighted with this worship as He watched Grandpa follow honest measurements, in the process teaching a little boy the way of godliness. The Bible says,

> Behold, to obey is better than sacrifice (1 Samuel 15:22).

> To do justice and judgment is more acceptable to the Lord than sacrifice (Proverbs 21:3).

Obedience is worship to God. God is worshiped and greatly delighted when His children willingly and lovingly obey His Word. "They that deal truly are his delight."

As Grandpa and Menno sacked wheat, God was delighted. He got still more delight out of seeing Grandpa teach a lesson that would influence his grandson's character for the rest of his life.

Church people employ many different forms and means of worship. Much emphasis is placed on style and liturgy. Some suggest using dance, drums, and noises to rouse up a spirit of worship. The ideas people come up with to worship are too lengthy to mention. The real worship of God gets lost in the shuffle of human effort. Obedience to God's teaching is true worship. Grandpa was worshiping God as he measured his wheat. "A just weight is his delight."

Suppose John, a church member, has an old clunker of a car with 250,000 miles and some rather noticeable pings in the engine. It uses so much oil there is no point in changing it. Because he doesn't want to spend much on repairs, he decides to get rid of it.

He has two options: Tell the truth about the car and accept a just and fair price for it or do a few cover-up cosmetics and get several hundred more out of it. The cover-up wouldn't cost much, and it may yield some dollars. Several cans of S.T.P. motor additive might quiet the ping and reduce the blue smoke when a potential buyer starts it up. If he sells it in the next 60 days, he can get it off his hands before the next inspection is due.

Let's say he chooses option two. That option comes easily because he remembers playing in the neighbor's barn while his father and grandfather sacked wheat they were buying. He heard Grandpa explain that if they round it up as high as it goes, after awhile they get a bushel free. So in goes the S.T.P. The ping is noticeably quieter. If one can help, two should be better. He cleans it up, notices the 56,000 miles on the odometer for the third time, puts it by the road with a For Sale sign that says "Runs good."

His potential customer stops and looks. How's the engine? "Runs good." Use oil? "A little." Actual mileage? "Yep—well actually it has turned over once."

As the inquirer drives away to take it for a spin, John

smiles to himself. That engine sounds pretty quiet, and it doesn't smoke much. I'm going to ask $400 for it. That's pretty good considering I'd have to pay $50 to have it hauled off if the engine blew.

Now comes the dealing. "What's your price?" "$400." "Can't afford that. How about $300?" "$350," says John. It's a deal.

The next Sunday John and his family are at his brother's house for Sunday dinner. While they wait for the call to gather at the table, John tells about his car deal. "The S.T.P. quieted the engine right down. The guy asked about the mileage. I told him it turned over once. He didn't ask more about it. I got $350 out of the old clunker. As this foreign-speaking guy drove off, I stuffed the money into my pocket and thought, 'Good riddance, hope I see neither again.' Me and S.T.P. pulled a good one." John is joined by a few others in a good chuckle.

Just then dinner is ready. The families with their children gather around the table. Mashed potatoes, roast beef, gravy, fresh-baked dinner rolls, fresh iced tea, with strawberry pie on the counter for dessert. John, would you please return thanks?

"Heavenly Father, we thank thee. . . ."

Wait a minute, what's going on here? Is God being worshiped? God saw the whole deal. He saw one of His people from a foreign land being ripped off. He heard the laughter about the deal. He got no delight out of the deal or the story. Will He now get delight out of the prayer? Go ahead and say it and stuff yourselves, but God is not delighted, nor did He receive worship out of the deal.

On the other hand, let's suppose John chooses option one: Tell the truth and take a fair price. He gets out all his belongings, tossing most of them into the trash. Then he sweeps out the dirt. "Doesn't look too bad. Lots of good memories. It did a good job climbing Pikes Peak. Took us to the West Coast—not a stitch of trouble."

The sign says "For sale—as is—make offer." A young fellow speaking broken English stops by. "Not much money. Need a car to get to my job. Have a wife and baby. Will it take me to my job?"

"It's seen it's best days. It does have 250,000 miles on it. Uses oil and has a ping in the engine as you can hear. I think it would run a while to get you to work and back. It might pass inspection if you put an additive in the oil. S.T.P might help. Can't guarantee it."

The little fellow smiles and says, "You think it will get me to my job and back, you take a hundred for it?" John thinks—suppose the engine does blow up and this guy would be stuck. Then he says, "Actually, it has very good tires that are worth something. I'll take $50 for it. If you have any real problem with it, let me know."

A shocked young man hands over three twenties. John leafs through the bills in his wallet till he finds a ten. The happy young fellow smiles as he takes the ten and the extra set of keys. Then his smile gets broader as they shake hands. "Thank you, my name is José. Tell me, I'm not used to this way of dealing. Why did you tell me about the engine noise? Why didn't you add the S.T.P.? That's the way many of my friends do. You could have gotten more money."

John hesitates slightly, then replies, "I'm a follower of Jesus Christ—a Christian. My guidebook teaches me that we should 'provide things honest in the sight of all men.'[4] We should 'walk honestly,' decently, behave properly, and put on the Lord Jesus Christ, and make no provision for the flesh.

"The Bible teaches that I should 'walk honestly toward them that are without' (1 Thessalonians 4:12). It also says: 'Whatsoever things are true, whatsoever things are honest,' these are the things I should think about (Philippians 4:8). I sure hope you get $50 worth of driving out of this car."

José drives off, leaving a trail of smoke as he goes. John goes back to mowing grass and prays, "God, let this car run for this fellow, and I pray that he will experience the Spirit of Truth in his heart."

Weeks later, he sees his old car in town; the driver gives him a hearty wave.

This is the kind of deal that delights God. It is the kind of transaction that brings worship to God. When you make this kind of deal, God is honored. "It has 250,000 miles on it, has a noise in the engine, S.T.P. may help, I can't guarantee it. I'll take $50 for it." That's the delightful language of worship to God.

Giving a testimony of faith in Jesus Christ and what the Scriptures teach brings great delight to God. I can imagine glory beams glistening from heaven when God's children use just weights and deal honestly. I can imagine an extra bright gleam of glory reaching God when His children testify of the grace and goodness of Jesus Christ.

Jesus said,

> Let your light so shine before men, that they may see your good works, and glorify your Father which is in heaven (Matthew 5:16).

> Herein is my Father glorified, that ye bear much fruit (John 15:8).

Truth, honesty, and integrity are streams of true worship that delight God. These are the acts of worship that glorify the Spirit of Truth, Jesus Christ our Savior and Lord.

Let us return to Menno Beachy and his grandfather. What would have happened if Grandpa had "heaped up" the container with all the wheat it would hold, and in the process explained to his grandson that if you heap it up you can get an extra half bushel for the price of two?

First, God would not have gotten delight out of that. Such actions are an abomination to Him. He would not have received glory.

Second, grandson Menno would have picked up a lesson on how to take advantage of people and get a little more for your money.

Third, that lesson would have begun the making of a character. That character likely would have developed a business lifestyle of "heaping it up" and getting an unfair edge on others. He would have been a candidate for "speaking lies in hypocrisy; having [his] conscience seared with a hot iron."[5]

Fourth, such an example could produce a man who would spend his life pleasing himself instead of God. He could easily have turned to a chronic, addictive lifestyle of cheating; one that would have required much disciplined training in righteousness to overcome.

Praise be to God, Grandpa provided a godly example that lives on and brings delight to God.

Persons who live honestly are a delight to God. Those whose word can be believed bring glory to the name of God. The expression "I'll lay my hand on a stack of Bibles and swear this is the truth" does not make an honest person.

God is delighted when we live honest lives that need no swearing of oaths to be believed. Jesus said,

> Again, ye have heard that it hath been said by them of old time, Thou shalt not forswear thyself, but shalt perform unto the Lord thine oaths: But I say unto you, Swear not at all; neither by heaven; for it is God's throne: Nor by the earth; for it is his footstool: neither by Jerusalem; for it is the city of the great King. Neither shalt thou swear by thy head, because thou canst not make one hair white or black. But let your communication be, Yea, yea; Nay, nay: for whatsoever is more than these cometh of evil (Matthew 5:33-37).

Swearing of oaths suggests that now you'll be truthful, because at other times you may not tell the truth. God is delighted to see His people live beyond the need for swearing an oath. Truly honest people need not place their hand on a Bible and swear to tell the truth.

God is delighted in people who "have denounced the hidden things of dishonesty."[6] He is so delighted that He has an eternal reward waiting for them. He is delighted to have honest followers whose names are written in the Lamb's Book of Life. He will reward those who have the Spirit of Truth with an eternal rest. That rest will be completely free of liars.

John writes of his vision of this new liar-free world:

> And I John saw the holy city, new Jerusalem, coming down from God out of heaven, prepared as a bride adorned for her husband. And I heard a great voice out of heaven saying, Behold, the tabernacle of God is with men, and he will dwell with them, and they shall be his people, and God himself shall be with them, and be their God. And God shall wipe away all tears from their eyes; and there shall be no more death, neither sorrow, nor crying, neither shall there be any more pain: for the former things are passed away (Revelation 21:2-4).

> And the city had no need of the sun, neither of the moon, to shine in it: for the glory of God did lighten it, and the Lamb is the light thereof (Revelation 21:23).

> And nothing unclean and no one who practices abomination and lying, shall ever come into it, but only those whose names are written in the

Lamb's book of life (Revelation 21:27, NASB).

What a reward God has for His children. They will be in the presence of the Truth, Jesus Christ. The father of lies and other liars will never be able to intrude or enter the new city. It pays to have the Spirit of Truth within and to walk in honesty before God.

Audrey Shank[7] told how her father taught her to put apples in a basket to sell them. She was to put the big apples in the bottom and pile them high and round on the top. The customer got more than a bushel of apples. That delighted God! Now her father is receiving heaped blessings in eternity as God delights in giving him rewards.

> Now the God of peace, that brought again from the dead our Lord Jesus, that great shepherd of the sheep, through the blood of the everlasting covenant, Make you perfect in every good work to do his will, working in you that which is well pleasing in his sight, through Jesus Christ; to whom be glory for ever and ever. Amen (Hebrews 13:20, 21).

> And the Lord make you to increase and abound in love one toward another, and toward all men, even as we do toward you: To the end he may stablish your hearts unblameable in holiness before God, even our Father, at the coming of our Lord Jesus Christ with all his saints (1 Thessalonians 3:12, 13).

> May the Spirit of Truth dwell in you and make you a

person of honesty and integrity, so that your good works will be a delight and an act of worship to God.

Then, when your good works and acts of obedient worship are completed here, may you be rewarded in God's presence for all eternity, where no one who practices lying will enter, but only those whose names are written in the Lamb's Book of Life.

Those who are born of the Spirit of Truth and practice honesty in this life delight God. They will be delighted with God's reward for all eternity.

---

1. Pritchard, Ray, *Names of the Holy Spirit*, Moody Press, 1995, p.178.
2. Also see Proverbs 15:3.
3. Beachy, Menno, *Grace Enough for My Life's Journey*, R.E.F. Typesetting and Publishing, p. 9.
4. Romans 12:17.
5. 1 Timothy 4:2.
6. 2 Corinthians 4:2.
7. Audrey Shank is the daughter of the late J. Ward Shank, a long-time bishop in Virginia and editor of *The Sword and Trumpet*.

Questions for Discussion

1. How does God respond when honesty rules our lives?
2. What example did Menno's grandfather give him?
3. How does God respond to our "worship" when conscious untruthfulness resides in us?
4. Truthfulness delights God! What other positive results issue from truthfulness? (Make as long a list as you can.)
5. What does swearing oaths imply about a person's usual truthfulness.
6. What kind of business behavior pleases God?
7. What reward awaits truthful people?

More Books by Simon Schrock

Has it ever occurred to you that God may have some thoughts concerning your wardrobe? Did you ever wonder what the Bible has to say about the subject of appearance?

What Shall the Redeemed Wear? addresses these questions and more by looking at what the Scriptures have to say concerning this important subject.

What Shall the Redeemed Wear?

• by Simon Schrock •

With Study Questions

Paperback - 120 pages

From Genesis to Revelation and generation to generation, God calls His people to be separated unto Him. Is personal appearance excluded from that call? Can one follow the fashions of this world and still have the approval of God?

You will find this book refreshingly honest, like a cool refreshing drink on a hot summer day. The clear, well-illustrated teaching of old truths is a breath of fresh air for those who are seeking relief from the endless merry-go-round of fashion that has so captivated many in the Christian world.

—Glenn Yoder
Bishop, Rosewood Fellowship, Middlebury, IN

Great for Group Studies
Quantity Discounts Available

To order, use the order form in back of this book

A Cyclorama of Encouragement

Follow the page by page cyclorama of encouragement.

Then the scene shifts to Stephen, the first martyr for Christ,[1] to the conversion of Saul on the road to Damascus,[2] and to John on the Isle of Patmos.[3]

We skip across the years of the church to the Reformation, noticing the severe persecution and martyrdom of the Anabaptists,[4] and right around to our day.

Write today's date in this space _____. This brings us near the time when the cyclorama will be full circle, when Jesus comes to bring His people home to Himself for eternity.

Right now there is a little space of grace called "today"   Grace   . When that space of

1. Acts 7:1–8:1   4. See *The Anabaptist Story* published by Wm. B. Eerdmans, Grand Rapids, Michigan
2. Acts 9:1-30
3. Revelation 1:9

24

"Anyone of any age will benefit from Schrock's message!"

‑anonymous

When Jesus died, the Apostle Peter threw in the towel. Thinking all his hopes and dreams were blasted, he said, "I go a fishing." But Jesus rose from the dead and handed Peter's towel back. Peter got the point. After years of serving, he said, "Put on the towel of humility." After reading this book, you too will be inspired to pick up and use that towel you were ready to throw!

To order, use the order form in back of this book

Order Form

To order, send this completed order form to:
Vision Publishers
P.O. Box 190
Harrisonburg, VA 22803
Fax: 540-437-1969
E-mail: orders@vision-publishers.com
www.vision-publishers.com

_____ _____
Name   Date

_____ _____
Mailing Address   Phone

_____ _____
City   State   Zip

Where Has Integrity Gone?   Qty. _____ x $3.99 each = _____

What Shall the Redeemed Wear? Qty. _____ x $5.99 each = _____

Don't Throw in the Towel   Qty. _____ x $3.99 each = _____

Price _____

Virginia residents add 5% sales tax _____

Ohio residents add applicable sales tax _____

Shipping & handling ___**$4.50**___

Grand Total _____

❏ Check #_____

❏ Money Order   ❏ Visa   **All Payments in US Dollars**

❏ MasterCard   ❏ Discover

Name on Card _____

Card # __|__|__|__| __|__|__|__| __|__|__|__| __|__|__|__|

3-digit code from signature panel __|__|__| Exp. Date __|__|__|__|

Thank you for your order!

For a complete listing of our books write for our catalog.
Bookstore inquiries welcome

Order Form

To order, send this completed order form to:
Vision Publishers
P.O. Box 190
Harrisonburg, VA 22803
Fax: 540-437-1969
E-mail: orders@vision-publishers.com
www.vision-publishers.com

_____ _____
Name   Date

_____ _____
Mailing Address   Phone

_____
City   State   Zip

Where Has Integrity Gone?   Qty. _____ x $3.99 each = _____

What Shall the Redeemed Wear? Qty. _____ x $5.99 each = _____

Don't Throw in the Towel   Qty. _____ x $3.99 each = _____

Price _____

Virginia residents add 5% sales tax _____

Ohio residents add applicable sales tax _____

Shipping & handling __**$4.50**__

Grand Total _____

❑ Check #_____

❑ Money Order   ❑ Visa   **All Payments in US Dollars**

❑ MasterCard   ❑ Discover

Name on Card _____

Card # __|__|__|__| __|__|__|__| __|__|__|__| __|__|__|__|

3-digit code from signature panel __|__|__| Exp. Date __|__|__|__|

Thank you for your order!

For a complete listing of our books write for our catalog.
Bookstore inquiries welcome

You Can Find Our Books at These Stores:

CALIFORNIA
Squaw Valley
   Sequoia Christian Books
   559/332-2606

COLORADO
Fruita
   Grand Valley Dry Goods
   970/858-1268

FLORIDA
Miami
   Alpha and Omega
   305/273-1263
Orlando
   Borders Books and Music
   407/826-8912

GEORGIA
Glennville
   Vision Bookstore
   912/654-4086
Montezuma
   The Family Book Shop
   478/472-5166

ILLINOIS
Arthur
   Arthur Distributor Company
   217/543-2166

   Clearview Fabrics and Books
   217/543-9091

   Miller's Dry Goods
   175-E County Road SO-N
Ava
   Pineview Books
   584 Bollman Road

INDIANA
Goshen
   Miller's Country Store
   574/642-3861

R And B's Kuntry Store
574/825-0191

Shady Walnut Grocery
574/862-2368
LaGrange
Pathway Bookstore
2580 North 250 West
Middlebury
   F and L Country Store
   574/825-7513

   Laura's Fabrics
   55140 County Road 43
Nappanee
   Little Nook Bookstore
   574/642-1347
Odon
   Dutch Pantry
   812/636-7922

   Schrock's Kountry Korner
   812/636-7842
Shipshewana
   E and S Sales
   260/768-4736
Wakarusa
   Maranatha Christian Bookstore
   574/862-4332

IOWA
Carson
   Refining Fires Books
   712/484-2214
Kalona
   Friendship Bookstore
   2357 540th Street SW

KANSAS
Hutchinson
   Gospel Book Store
   620/662-2875

**Our books may also be found on many
Choice Books bookracks and Lantern Books bookracks**

Moundridge
Gospel Publishers
620/345-2532

KENTUCKY
Manchester
Lighthouse Ministries
606/599-0607
Stephensport
Martin's Bookstore
270/547-4206

LOUISIANA
Belle Chasse
Good News Bookstore
504/394-3087

MARYLAND
Grantsville
Shady Grove Market and Fabrics
301/895-5660
Hagerstown
J. Millers Gospel Store
240/675-0383
Landover
Integrity Church Bookstore
301/322-3311
Oakland
Countryside Books and More
301/334-3318
Silver Spring
Potomac Adventist Bookstore
301/572-0700

Union Bridge
Hege's Catalog Store
410/775-7643

MICHIGAN
Burr Oak
Chupp's Herbs and Fabric
269/659-3950
Charlotte

Meadow Ridge Woodcrafts LLC
517/543-8680
Clare
Colonville Country Store
989/386-8686
Snover
Country View Store
989/635-3764

MISSOURI
Advance
Troyer's Grocery
573/722-3406
La Russell
Schrock's Kountry Korner
417/246-5351
Rutledge
Zimmerman's Store
660/883-5766
Seymour
Byler Supply & Country Store
417/935-4522
Shelbyville
Windmill Ridge Bulk Foods
4100 Highway T
Versailles
Excelsior Bookstore
573/378-1925
Weatherby
Country Variety Store
816/449-2932
Windsor
Rural Windsor Books and
Variety
660/647-2705

NEW MEXICO
Farmington
Lamp and Light Publishers
505/632-3521

NEW YORK

**Our books may also be found on many
Choice Books bookracks and Lantern Books bookracks**

Seneca Falls
Sauder's Store
315/568-2673

NORTH CAROLINA
Blanch
Yoder's Country Market
336/234-8072
Greensboro
Borders Books and Music
336/218-0662
Raleigh
Borders Books and Music #365
919/755-9424

NORTH DAKOTA
Mylo
Lighthouse Bookstore
701/656-3331

OKLAHOMA
Miami
Eicher's Country Store
918/540-1871

OHIO
Berlin
Christian Aid Ministries
330/893-2428

Gospel Book Store
330/893-2523
Brinkhaven
Little Cottage Books
740/824-3808
Dalton
Little Country Store
330/828-8411
Fredricksburg
Faith-View Books
330/674-4129
Leetonia

Tinkling Spring Country Store
330/482-4592
Mesopotamia
Eli Miller's Leather Shop
440/693-4448
Middlefield
S & E Country Store
440/548-2347
Millersburg
Country Furniture & Bookstore
330/893-4455
Plain City
Deeper Life Bookstore
614/873-1199
Seaman
Keim Family Market
937/386-9995
Sugarcreek
JSR Fabric and Shoes
330/852-2721

The Gospel Shop
330/852-4223

Troyer's Bargain Store
2101 County Road 70

OREGON
Estacada
Bechtel Books
530/630-4606
Halsey
Shoppe of Shalom
541/369-2369

PENNSYLVANIA
Amberson
Scroll Publishing Co.
717/349-7033
Belleville
Yoder's Gospel Book Store
717/483-6697
Chambersburg

**Our books may also be found on many
Choice Books bookracks and Lantern Books bookracks**

Burkholder Fabrics
717/369-3155

Pearson's Pasttimes
717/267-1415

Denver
Weaver's Store
717/445-6791

Ephrata
Clay Book Store
717/733-7253

Conestoga Bookstore
717/354-0475

Home Messenger Library &
Bookstore
717/351-0218

Ken's Educational Joys
717/351-8347

Gordonville
Ridgeview Bookstore
717/768-7484

Greencastle
Country Dry Goods
717/593-9661

Guys Mills
Christian Learning Resource
814/789-4769

Leola
Conestoga Valley Bookbindery
717/656-8824

Lewisburg
Crossroads Gift and Bookstore
570/522-0536

McVeytown
Penn Valley Christian Retreat
717/899-5000

Meadville
Gingerich Books and Notions
814/425-2835

Monroe

Border's Books and Music
412/374-9772

Mount Joy
Mummau's Christian Bookstore
717/653-6112

Myerstown
Witmer's Clothing
717/866-6845

Newville
Corner Store
717/776-4336

Rocky View Bookstore
717/776-7987

Parkesburg
Brookside Bookstore
717/692-4759

Quarryville
Countryside Bargains
717/528-2360

Shippensburg
Mt. Rock Bookstore
717/530-5726

Springboro
Chupp's Country Cupboard
814/587-3678

SOUTH CAROLINA
Barnwell
The Genesis Store
803/541-6109

North Charleston
World Harvest Ministries
843/554-7960

Summerville
Manna Christian Bookstore
843/873-4221

Sumter
Anointed Word Christian Bookstore
803/494-9894

**Our books may also be found on many
Choice Books bookracks and Lantern Books bookracks**

TENNESSEE

Crossville
MZL English Book Ministry
931/277-3686

Troyer's Country Cupboard
931/277-5886

Deer Lodge
Mt. Zion Literature Ministry
931/863-8183

Paris
Miller's Country Store
731/644-7535

Sparta
Valley View Country Store
931/738-5465

TEXAS

Kemp
Heritage Market and Bakery
903/498-3366

Seminole
Nancy's Country Store
432/758-9162

VIRGINIA

Bristow
The Lighthouse Books
703/530-9039

Dayton
Books of Merit
540/879-2628

Mole Hill Books & More
540/867-5928

Rocky Cedars Enterprises
540/879-9714

Harrisonburg
Christian Light Publications
540/434-0768

McDowell
Sugar Tree Country Store
540/396-3469

Rural Retreat
Bender's Fabrics
276/686-4793

Woodbridge
Mennonite Maidens
703/622-3018

WASHINGTON

North Bonneville
Moore Foundation
800/891-5255

WEST VIRGINIA

Renick
Yoders' Select Books
304/497-3990

WISCONSIN

Dalton
Mishler's Country Store
West 5115 Barry Rd.

Granton
Mayflower Country Store
715/238-7988

South Wayne
Pilgrim's Pantry
608/439-1064

CANADA

BRITISH COLUMBIA

Burns Lake
Wildwood Bibles and Books
250/698-7451

Montney
Janice Martin Books
250/327-3231

MANITOBA

Arborg
Sunshine Christian Books
204/364-3135

**Our books may also be found on many
Choice Books bookracks and Lantern Books bookracks**

ONTARIO

Aylmer
Mennomex
519/773-2002

Brunner
Country Cousins
519/595-4277

Lighthouse Books
519/595-4500

Floradale
Hillcrest Home Baking and Dry
Goods
519/669-1381

Linwood
Living Waters Christian Bookstore
519/698-1198

Mount Forest
Shady Lawn Books
519/323-2830

Newton
Canadian Family Resources
519/595-7585

**Our books may also be found on many
Choice Books bookracks and Lantern Books bookracks**